Neither the Charm
Nor the Luck

MAJ. GENERAL JOHN SULLIVAN

KARL F. STEPHENS MD

Major–General John Sullivan

Neither the Charm Nor the Luck

Outskirts Press, Inc.
Denver, Colorado

To My Wife, Doris—
Thanks

Contents

Maps

" 'SULLIVAN' WAS HERE "

Montreal

NY

VT

NH

16

17

MA

15

3

CT

13

PA

14

NJ

6

12   8

11   7   9

10

MD

18

1. NEW HAMPSHIRE : CHAPTERS 1 & 13
2. PHILADELPHIA : CHAPTERS 3 & 13
3. BOSTON : CHAPTER 4
4. CANADA : CHAPTER 5
5. CROWN POINT : CHAPTER 5
6. LONG ISLAND : CHAPTER 6
7. TRENTON : CHAPTER 7
8. PRINCETON : CHAPTER 7
9. STATEN ISLAND : CHAPTER 8
10. BRANDYWINE : CHAPTER 9
11. GERMANTOWN : CHAPTER 10
12. VALLEY FORGE : CHAPTER 10
13. RHODE ISLAND : CHAPTER 11
14. WYOMING, PA : CHAPTER 12
15. NEWTOWN, NY : CHAPTER 12
16. GENEVA, NY : CHAPTER 12
17. GENESEO, NY : CHAPTER 12
18. ANNAPOLIS,MD : CHAPTER 13

Preface

In 1991, while writing an article about Rhode Island's Revolutionary War "Black Regiment", I became enthralled with the American commander at the Battle of Rhode Island, Major–General John Sullivan. It seemed as if he were the "Kilroy" of his war. Read about most incidents or battles, minor or pivotal, and there is his name, mentioned in some way. Speak of him to a contemporary, and they claim him for their locale.

A son in Pennsylvania daily passed a roadside plaque which informed passersby that General Sullivan had been there at the Battle of Brandywine. While visiting in Elmira, N.Y., my brother–in–law apprised me of the fact that the famous Battle of Newtown had been fought in the area–and General Sullivan was the American commander. Friends in New Hampshire had the New Hampshire Division of Historical Resources inundate me with Sullivan references, making sure I remembered Sullivan was their "native son". I even had a cousin who felt his fond memories of summer in Sullivan County, N.Y., made him an acquaintance of the general. (Though Sullivan County is named for General Sullivan, neither my cousin—nor, it seems, anyone else—knows exactly why.)

However, even more striking than Sullivan's omnipresence is that, despite this, he has never been one of those personages invoked at the mention of the Revolutionary War. While it makes him, to me, even more intriguing, what probably accounts for this disregard is General Sullivan's also being one of the more controversial figures in American history, never mind the Revolutionary War.

"Irish, but with neither the proverbial charm nor the luck",[1] is one of the more temperate descriptions of him by his detractors. "Singularly unattractive", "endlessly carping and whining", and "agent of disaster" are some others.

Yet, just as did Grant with Lincoln and Patton with Eisenhower, though his vilifiers were legion, Sullivan enjoyed the confidence of the person who mattered most, the one in charge.

George Washington, though realizing Sullivan had a "little tincture of vanity and an over–desire of being popular", also looked on him as "active, spirited, and zealously attach'd (sic) to the cause"–someone he could count on to get the job done. (As was Patton, the enemy considered Sullivan to be "the most active general" they were facing.)

While stimulated by Sullivan's uniqueness to write about him, I also felt that, primarily because of the efforts of Thomas C. Amory and Otis G. Hammond, there was nothing new I could add to the Sullivan lore. But, I realized that what I personally missed while delving into the subject–and what would be appropriate for a competitor

---

1   Ketchum, Richard M. "Men of the Revolution XIII". American Heritage, 25:05, Aug.74, p.31.

like Sullivan–was a more informal work, one that would entertain his "hot–stove–league" followers. I have tried to write it.

To satisfy another personal preference, an attempt has been made to intersperse, within the text, not only ample maps–but at the appropriate places.

Early Years:
Chapters 1,2, and 3.

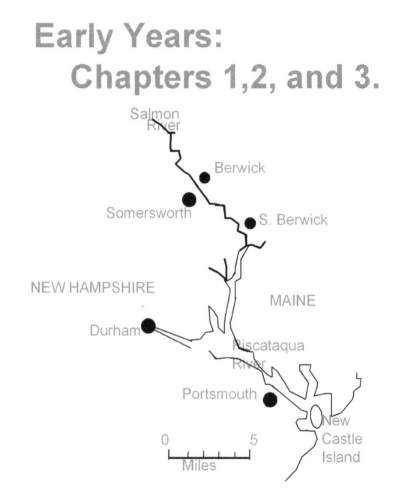

CHAPTER **One**

Family History

In 1723, two redemptioners from Ireland, John Sullivan and Margery Browne, settled on the banks of the Salmon–Falls River, which separates southern New Hampshire and Maine. Spirited and remarkable individually, their union in marriage, approximately 15 years later, would provide much spice to the stew of America.

Master John Sullivan, the father of the General John Sullivan who is our protagonist, came from a long line of Irish warriors [2], as is exemplified by his father, Major Phillip Sullivan. The latter, in true Irish fashion, not only fought the English until the bitter end; but when, as part of the garrison of Limerick, he was forced to surrender in 1691 to William of Orange, he chose exile in France rather than pledge an oath of allegiance to the English government. While in France he had a duel with a French officer—why,

---

2   Those so inclined are welcome to work their way through the exhaustive chronicling of this by Thomas C, Amory in The Military Services and Public Life of Major–General John Sullivan, Boston, M A: Wiggin and Lunt,1868.pp266–284.

we do not know; but one can only speculate that, like his grandson , he was "overly sensitive"[3]–sustaining a wound that was to account for his being, according to his son's later statement, "short–lived".

Master John Sullivan, however, was part of a "skip generation" in this martial legacy, serving as a school master between his father, Major Phillip, and the four of his sons who served as officers in the armed forces.

Although not a military man like his father–evidently he was originally destined for the priesthood–Master John did share the family antipathy regarding relations with the English. After receiving a seminary education on the continent–endowed for him by his family in more prosperous times–he returned to Ireland, only to encounter "persecutions and discouragements" that prompted him to emigrate to America in 1723.

(Of course, while linking his emigration with "efforts to restore the Stuarts" seems to be favored by the Sullivan's' primary biographer, Thomas C. Amory,[4]one has to wonder about the simultaneous emigration of Margery Browne. She was to become his wife; and she might also have been considered "beneath his station" by his mother who, while now impoverished, was, after all, the relative of an Earl!)

Once in America, "the advantages of a good education" quickly served Master John well. His ability to not only speak several languages, but his being a good

---

3   One of those interesting "sidelights to history": In 1778 the grandson, General John Sullivan, came close to having a duel with another French officer, the Marquis de Lafayette.(See Chapter 11).

4   Perhaps because he was a great grandson of the Sullivan in question! His work: Amory, Thomas C. The Military Services and Public Life of Major–General John Sullivan. Boston, Mass: Wiggin and Lunt, 1868. is the source of most of this early biographical information.

mathematician, attracted the attention of a local clergyman, one Doctor Moody. Doctor Moody purchased Sullivan's freedom for him, and arranged for him to become the schoolmaster for the parish in Summersworth (Somersworth), N.H., in 1738, a vocation he continued in the area until in his 90s. (He died at age 105.)

Now established himself, Master Sullivan at this point bought the freedom of Margery Browne, who "had come with him to this country as a child." Soon after her emancipation, and her having "grown up to womanhood", he married her.

Margery Sullivan was said by contemporaries to possess both great "personal beauty" and "force of character". Evidently the latter was a euphemism for what some considered "vanity and a violent temper"; and on at least one occasion her schoolmaster husband, though descended from Irish chieftains, fled to the environs of Boston to seek sanctuary from her "rash and unadvised speech and behaviour (sic)".

In any case, while not as much is known of her background as is known of her husband's, all agree that to her, as well as to the father, "may be ascribed the energy and vigor which made their children distinguished."

Master John and Margery Sullivan had six children, five boys and one girl; and it is quite a legacy that they left to America.

Mary, the only daughter, became, within a century, the ancestress of a Lieutenant–Governor, a Governor, and a U.S. Senator–not to mention a Consul at Bermuda.

The oldest boy, Benjamin, served in the British Navy, of all things; and all that seems to be said about him is that, before the separation of the colonies from the mother country, he was lost at sea.

However, the other four boys took an active part in the Revolutionary War—on the American side.

Daniel, the oldest of the four, became a captive of the British. In the tradition of his grandfather, he refused to take an oath of allegiance to the king to gain his freedom, and subsequently died as the result of being incarcerated in a British prison ship. (See Chapter 13.)

James was evidently the only one to serve in the non-combatant role of "statesman".

Eben (Ebenezer), the youngest, came close to being burned alive by the Iroquois Indians while serving as a volunteer hostage after The Battle of the Cedars, May 1776. He was eventually exchanged, in 1778, and resumed active service in the Continental Army, where he rose to the rank of major.

Finally, as if this were not enough a record of accomplishment and bravery for one family, there is the most remarkable son of all, Major-General John Sullivan of the American Revolutionary Army!

CHAPTER **TWO**

Early Manhood

General John Sullivan was born to Master John and Margery Sullivan in Somersworth, New Hampshire, on February 17, 1740. Not long after, Master Sullivan moved his family across the Salmon Falls River to an 80 acre farm on the bank of the river in South Berwick, Maine; so, although often described as "the son of a poor teacher", one has the feeling that John and his siblings were amply provided for during their childhood.

One thing their schoolmaster father was definitely able to provide them with was an education that was far better than most in the area received. The overall level of general information, acquaintance with classical literature, and ability to write of all of his children was comparable to the "collegiate culture" of the day.

Sullivan then followed up on this advantage by applying, as a teen–ager, to "split the wood, take care of the house, and attend to the gardening" at the home of a busy Portsmouth, N.H. lawyer, Samuel Livermore, in exchange for the chance to "read a little law" under his instruction. Given the opportunity, Sullivan proved to be an intelligent and ambitious student–worker; and the story told of his "graduation" to the full–time study of law is quite believable, in light of his future career.

Sullivan would study in Mr. Livermore's library when the lawyer was absent. He was doing so one evening when the winner of a fight in town, who was now being sued by the loser for assault and battery, arrived at Livermore's office seeking legal assistance for his defense in the case, which was now to be heard before Deacon Penhallow. In what the future would show to be characteristic fashion, after hearing the defendant's request, Sullivan assured him that he could win the case for him in Livermore's place. Leaving word in the Livermore kitchen where he was going, he headed off with his first client to do so.

While the trial was going on, Mr. Livermore returned to be told his kitchen worker was off to Deacon Penhallow's to defend a suit. "His curiosity excited," Livermore slipped unobserved in to a room at the Deacon's, next to where the trial was taking place. Sullivan, with "good tact," (which might be said to be un–characteristic), "native talent", and knowledge of the law won the case–and made sure he collected here his first court fee. Without then revealing his presence for the trial, Livermore slipped home. The next morning he called Sullivan into his library, to inform him that the kitchen was no longer the place for him.

So, at this time, Sullivan started his own practice. He also took on the added responsibility of starting a family. In 1760, he married Lydia Remick Worster of Kittery, Maine. (One senses she was a "homebody", more interested in family than "worldly" things, and brought stability to the union.)

Sullivan started his practice in Berwick; then, around 1763, he moved to Durham, N.H. Durham's 1,200 residents of the time were said to be devoted to "peaceable pursuits of rural life", and were not too happy to see their first lawyer in town arrive, feeling they did not require lawyers , who only "fomented litigation for their own purposes and craftily devoured the substance of their neighbors ".   Evidently the ambitious Sullivan quickly proved their concerns were well founded. Described as "somewhat litigious", with all its negative connotations, he not only soon had many in town blaming him for their financial problems; but, within two years of his arrival, he pretty much had the town divided into pro—and anti—Sullivan factions.

(His facile use of legal language—i.e. ability to obfuscate—would also be enough to infuriate people, if the following letter is any example:

[John Sullivan to Capt. Wallingford]
Durham October 15th 1771
Sir I hear that there is Some Expression in the Reasons of appeal filed by me in behalf of your mother which give you some offence which I Declare I never meant however great the provocation might be which I Received. The provocation I beg Leave to mention which is as follows Namely when you applied to me at Deacon Leightons & I Refused Your money, I then told you that I would wait on Mrs. Wallingford the Next Day & get her to Consent to what you then Said you Desired which was to Take a Joint Administration with her which I accordingly did & persuaded her to Consent & you not being at Home I Left word with

your Lady to Desire you to appear at Portsmouth on the Fryday (sic) then next which you absolutely refused. All this I did at your Request & she (Mrs. Wallingford) well knows that I neither received fee or Reward for my Trouble and I have received no money from her Even to this Day Except a Trifle to pay the cost of appealing &c which I told her I did not receive as a fee but would Account with her for it when I had paid the Charges out of the Same—now Sir please to Consider whether putting me upon Such an Errand and Leaving me to be Laughed at for Thus being Imposed upon was not a very great affront but Notwithstanding all this I never had any thought of Returning the affront Nor is there one word in the Reason of Appeal that Looks Like it. Indeed it is there said that you had not Capacity to Transact the Necessary Business in Selling your fathers Estate which cant possibly be understood as want of Natural abilities or Capacity by any person acquainted with the English Language for why do we Ever add the word Natural to the word Capacity. Surely it must be to Convey Some Idea that the word Capacity alone would not as for Instance to Say that a man has not Capacity to do a certain thing or Transact a Certain piece of Business Implies only an unacquaintedness with it. But if we mean to Reflect upon his natural powers of Mind we say he has not a Natural Capacity for it. I should not take it as an affront if any person was to Say that I had not Capacity to Rule a Nation or Command an Army in Time of Battle Though perhaps some have acted in both Stations to whom Nature has not been more Liberal in her gifts than She has been to me nor should I look upon it as any Reflection upon my Natural Capacity for not having turned my thoughts on Either. I cannot well properly be Said to be Capable of Acting in

Either but if a person was to say that I had not Natural Capacity to Act in Either Station I would then Reflect on my Natural powers of mind nor can you possibly suppose it as a Reflection if I was to say you have not Capacity to preach a Sermon or plead Law although I well know there are many who do both whose natural powers are not superiour (sic) to yours. If you will only Consult Doctor Tillotson You will find he uses the word in the Same Sense as the word Qualified is used & to Convey the Same Idea. Cole in his Latin Dictionary under the word Capax from which the word Capacity is Derived says it means a man's understanding a thing well—he I suppose understood both Latin and English. So unless there be some persons who understand English better than the best English writers To Convince me to the Contrary I shall Suppose that the Word there used only Implies that you are not in every Respect Qualified to Settle the Affairs of the Estate without calling in assistance & I doubt not you are well Convinced of that your Self & if the word there used will not bear this Construction I Confess I am Mistaken in my English & have not at present Capacity to Discover where the Error Lies. I hope Sir you will See by what I have said on the Subject that no affront was Intended for Every thing of that Sort was Ever the aversion of Sir your Humble Servant. [5]" [Sic])

The first recorded skirmish in the battle caused by antipathy to Sullivan was in February, 1766. "Collisions" began to occur between Sullivan proponents and opponents. As these became more serious, with resultant casualties, a truce was finally called. It was next decided

---

5   Hammond, Otis G. Letters and Papers of Major-General John Sullivan. Volume One. Concord, N.H. New Hampshire Historical Society, 1930.pp 39–41

a particular dispute should be settled "the old fashioned way"—with a fight between Sullivan and a champion chosen from amongst his opponents. However, the next problem for Sullivan's enemies arose when they realized none of them was a match for Sullivan, "who possessed great physical strength".

Sullivan's younger brother, James, who was now studying law under John, solved this quandary for them by requesting to do battle for the lawyer's team. The encounter then took place; and brother James up–held the Sullivan name by winning.

Sullivan's great–grandson would like us to believe that, at this point, the townspeople acquiesced to the " result of the ordeal", and from then on placed only confidence in Sullivan. However, the records show this encounter did not end the war.

Only four months later, in June , 1766, Sullivan complained that a mob fired into his house and threatened to burn it down; although his antagonists claim they only wanted to get at all the " writs and notes of hand" Sullivan possessed.

Next, in June, 1766, they tried to beat Sullivan at his own game. (One wonders if another lawyer arrived, sensing an opportunity!) They took their complaint regarding his "oppressive and extortive behaviour (sic)" to the General Court, claiming "he with a view of making his fortune, out of the ruin of the poor harmless people, taking of them unreasonable fees...set himself up to the highest bidder, for to plead a case before a justice".[6] Their petitions asked for an end to his suits; but, there were others—probably the

6   Whittemore, Charles P.A General of the Revolution.. New York and London: Columbia University Press,1961.p.5.

winners in those suits–who described him as beneficent, and the petition was dismissed... Sullivan promptly sued for libel (!)–but was unsuccessful this time. Whether in spite of, or because of, all this publicity, Sullivan's practice began to prosper. (It was, perhaps, not so much due to any emergent fondness for Sullivan as it was for the realization–still known today–that, " while he may be a real S.O.B., I want him to be my S.O.B.") More and more, as brother James wrote, "his clients flock like the bees to their cell (and I hope come stored with honey for the same)."[7]

Furthermore, as John Adams wrote to his wife in 1774, Sullivan was starting to "make estates by law". Adams, obviously impressed with–and sounding a little envious of– Sullivan, goes on to say : "John Sullivan, who is placed at Durham, in New Hampshire, is younger , both in years and practice than I am. He began with nothing, but is now said to be worth ten thousand pounds, lawful money...He has a fine stream of water, with an excellent corn–mill, saw– mill, fulling–mill, scythe–mill, and others–in all six mills, which are both his delight and his profit. As he has earned cash in his business at the bar, he has taken opportunities to purchase farms of his neighbors, who wanted to sell and move out further in to the woods, at an advantageous rate, and in this way has been growing rich".[8]

As Sullivan grew rich, his family also grew. John and Lydia's first child, Margery, died in infancy; but between 1763 and 1771 they had another daughter and three

---

7   Hammond, Otis G. Letters and Papers of Major–General John Sullivan. Volume One. Concord, N.H.: New Hampshire Historical Society, 1930.p.41.
8   Amory, Thomas C. The Military Services and Public Life of Major–General John Sullivan Boston, Mass.: Wiggin and Lunt, 1868. P.294.

sons: Lydia, John, James, and George. In 1775 their last child was born. She was also named Margery; but, as if the name brought bad luck, she died at age two.

With his fortune made, and with success bringing respect, Sullivan became more and more active in the sphere where he would earn his place in history: the military and politics, with the local militia being an amalgam of the two. In this regard, Adams also noted : "Under the smiles and auspices of Governor Wentworth, he has been promoted in the civil and military way, so that he is treated with great respect ".[9]

---

9   Ibid

Political and Military Beginnings

Today, while we revere men such as John Adams and Thomas Jefferson for their contributions to the Declaration of Independence, it is consistent with Sullivan's lot that no one speaks of his work in laying the foundation for it.

Although awarded a Major's commission in the militia (2nd Regiment of Foot) by Governor Wentworth, in 1772, Sullivan, instead, entered formal politics, as a representative from Durham to the Provincial Assembly of New Hampshire, in the spring of 1774. Shortly thereafter, on 21Jul74, he became the first person chosen—by New Hampshire's First Provincial Congress, meeting at Exeter— to represent New Hampshire in the U.S. Congress. (He was reappointed 25Jan75.) On 10 Aug 74, along with Nathaniel Folsom of Exeter, the second delegate, Sullivan left for the First Continental Congress in Philadelphia.

From the beginning, Sullivan was an active member of the "warm" faction in Congress, favoring independence. He was immediately named to head the committee addressing the grievances of the people. John Adams was to note the later significance of his excellent legal and literary work in that regard:

"The committee of violation of rights reported a set of articles which were drawn by Mr. John Sullivan of New Hampshire, and these two declarations, the one of rights and the other of violations, which are printed in the journals of Congress for 1774, were two years afterwards recapitulated in the Declaration of Independence on the 4th of July, 1776."!!¹⁰

On 14 Oct 74, Congress adopted the "Declaration of Rights and Grievances" and concluded with a statement of determination by Congress to enter into a non–importation, non–exportation, and non–consumption association. This conformed with Sullivan's claim that power to regulate internal policy rested in the individual provincial legislatures–and ran counter to the conservative Joseph Galloway's plan of union, that accepted British hegemony, fanning Galloway's fears that it hinted at independency. (Galloway was to ultimately go over to the British side.)

On Sullivan's return to New Hampshire, he immediately set to work having the association approved, which the Second Provincial Congress eventually did, in late January,1775. Also occurring at this time—and would prove to be of even more significance for America's successful outcome—Sullivan began his active military role in the Revolution–as a leader of "the first act of armed rebellion", in December, 1774.

An order of the British King and Council prohibit-

---

10   Hammond, Otis G. Letters and Papers of Major–General John Sullivan Volume One Concord, N.H.: New Hampshire Historical Society, 1930. p.9

ing military stores from being sent to America alarmed Sullivan, and spurred him to action. On the nights of 14 and 15 December 74, Sullivan, along with Captain John Langdon, directed two raids targeting Fort William and Mary situated on Newcastle Island, at the mouth of the Piscataqua River, utilizing the militia he had been training. Some powder was seized the night of the 14th. On the 15th, Sullivan first engaged in some duplicity with his former patron, Governor John Wentworth. Sullivan agreed to send his men away, if Wentworth would assure him that no British would be called. However, after being sent away, the men of the militia just happened to gather at the Bell Tavern, where Sullivan just happened to be buying the drinks. After an evening's entertainment, at about 10:30 PM, Sullivan led a convivial band across the water to the fort, and seized the cannon and munitions there, before British ships could secure them. Sullivan, with the help of his law clerks and his hired man, next managed to transport most of the stores to Durham, evidently by means of a team of horses pulling it by barge up the river—with Sullivan et. al. chopping through the ice when necessary. In Durham it was hidden—partly under the pulpit of the meetinghouse—until later taken by Sullivan to Boston, where it was used in the Battle of Bunker Hill.

Shortly after those forays, on 24 Dec 74, "A Watchman" sent out a press release addressed "To the Inhabitants of British America". Its writer used his conversance with the classics to make clear to all throughout the country what actuated this first direct act of hostility:

"Friends and countrymen At a time, when Ministerial Tyrants Threaten a people with the Total Loss of their Liberties; Supineness and Inattention on their part will ren-

der that Ruin which their Enemies have designed for them unavoidable. A striking Instance of this we have in the History of the Carthaginians: That brave people notwithstanding they had Surrendered up three hundred Hostages to the Romans upon a promise of being Restored to their former Liberties; found themselves Instantly Invaded by the Roman Army. Roused by this unexpected procedure; they sent Deputies to know the Occasion of this Extraordinary Manuvre (sic). They were told That they must Deliver up all their Arms to the Romans and then they should peaceable Enjoy their Liberties upon their Compliance with this Requisition ; Marcius (one of the Roman Consuls) thus addressed them;' we are well pleased with these first Instances of your obedience and Therefore cannot help Congratulating you upon them; I have now but one thing more to require of you in the name of the Roman people: I will therefore without further preamble plainly Declare to you an Order on which the safety of your Republic the preservation of your Goods your lives and Liberties depend. Rome Requires that you abandon your City which we are Commanded to Level with the ground; you may build yourselves another where you please provided it be Ten miles from the Sea and without walls or fortifications, a little Courage and Resolution will Get the better of the affection which attaches us to Old habitations and is founded more in habit than in Reason.' The Consternation of the Carthaginian Deputies at hearing this Horrid Treacherous Speech is Not to be Expressed. Some Swooned away, others burst forth into Cries and Lamentations; nor were even the Roman soldiers who were present unmoved at the affecting scene. 'These sudden fits (said the Base, Inhuman Consuls) will wear off by Degrees. Time & Necessity

Teaches the most unfortunate, to bear their Calamities with patience; The Carthaginians when they recover their sences (sic) will Choose to Obey.'

Although the Carthaginians, after this made a noble and Manly Resistance yet the surrender of their Arms, proved the Destruction of that City, which had so often Contended with Rome, for the Empire of the world.

Equally Inexcusable with the Carthaginians will the Americans be, if they suffer the Tyrants who are Endeavouring to Enslave them to possess themselves of all their Forts Castles ammunition and warlike stores; what reason can be given by them for such Cowardly and Pusillanimous Conduct ? Perhaps it may be said that 'there yet remains Some Gleam of hope, that the British Ministry may do us Justice; Restore us to our Liberties; and Repeal those oppressive acts which now hand over America; and was this even probable it would hardly Justify such a Conduct. But what foundation have we for such hope? If this be the Intention of the Ministry, is a formidable Fleet and numerous Army necessary to Bring it about? Could they not have given up their plan for Enslaving America without soliciting and finally obtaining an order to prohibit the Importation of warlike stores into the Colonies? Does this Speak the Language of peace and Reconciliation; or does it not rather Speak that of war Tumult and Desolation? And shall we like the Carthaginians peaceably surrender our arms to our Enemies in hopes of obtaining in Return the Liberties we have so long Contended for? Be not Deceived my Countrymen, should the Ministry ever prevail upon you to make that Base and Infamous surrender they will then tell you in the Language of the Haughty and Inhumane Marcius, what those Liberties are, which they will in future suffer you to enjoy; and Endeavour to perswade (sic) you that when you have recovered your Sences (sic) you will Choose to obey. Is it possible that any person among us thinks of making a Submission to the Several powers which now claim a Right to Rule over us? If so Let him take a view of the situation he and his American Brethren must be in: We all acknowledge our submission to the authority of our provincial Legislature in the same manner as the people in Great Britain acknowledge the power of Parliament over them; because the assemblies here and Parliament there are Composed in part of persons Elected by the people & who are liable for any misconduct to be Excluded by them from ever acting again as their Representatives and where the people have this Constitutional Check upon their Rulers; Slavery can never be introduced.' But (says the famous Mr. Lock) whenever a power Exists in a state over which the people have no Control, the people are Compleatly Inslaved (sic); if this be the Case what shall we say to the Claim of parliament to Legislate for us in all Cases whatsoever? To the Mandates of a Minister of State, which so often have superseded (sic) the Laws of the Colony Legislatures although assented to by his Majesty? or to the Late order of the King and Council prohibiting the Importation of warlike stores into the Colonies ? & who by the same Colour of Right, may whenever they please prohibit the Importation of any or even Every other article? These are undoubtedly Such powers as we have no Check upon or Controul (sic) over, powers Similar to those which have spread Tyranny and Oppression over three quarters of the Globe:& if we Tamely submit to their authority, will soon Accomplish that slavery which they have Long been Endeavouring to bring upon America.

I am far from wishing Hostilities to Commence on the part of America. But still hope that no person will, at this Important Crisis be unprepared to act in his own Defence (sic); should he by necessity be Driven thereto, and I must here beg Leave to Recommend to the Consideration of the people on this Continent whether when we are by an Arbitrary Decree prohibited the having arms & Ammunition by Importation we have not, by the Law of self preservation a right to Sieze (sic) upon those within our power in Order to Defend the Liberties which God and Nature have given to us; Especially at this time when several of the Colonies are Involved in a Dangerous war with the Indians and must if this Inhumane order has the Designed Effect fall a prey to those Savage Barbarians who have so often Deluged this Land in Blood."[11](Sic)

Wentworth, incensed, especially with Sullivan, whom he knew to be the instigator of the trouble, was also frustrated. His reflex inclination was to apprehend Sullivan and consign him to England; but, he also knew the local political climate well enough to realize an attempt to do so would rally the populace to Sullivan's assistance. (A proclamation calling for the arrest of the perpetrators was already being ignored.) He even shied from immediately dismissing the militia officers who had participated in the raid, fearing it would martyrize them.

Eventually, in February 1775, Wentworth did revoke the commissions of Sullivan and the other leaders of the December irruption. But there are some accounts that Sullivan and others had already burned their commissions

11 Hammond, Otis G. Letters and Papers of Major–General John Sullivan. Volume One. Concord, N.H. New Hampshire Historical Society, 1930.pp50–53.

at a public bonfire, as a show of defiance; and, in any case, it certainly did not deter Sullivan from continuing to train a military company—much to the consternation of "Monitor", who wrote to the New Hampshire Gazette on March 17,1775:

"....In the first Place the Appointment of all Military Officers, whether for a Day, a Week or a month, is the sole Right of the King, or of those deriving Authority from him, and (to treat the Matter in the most moderate Terms) it is a very improper Step for any Body of Men, to assume that Power to themselves upon any Occasion or Pretence whatsoever.

The Laws of the Province require the Militia to be drawn forth to learn the Military Exercise four Times a Year, and no more; Mr. Sullivan may probably tell us, that this new modeled Company does not come under this Limitation, yet I presume he will not deny but that the Meeting of any Part of the Militia, and these People declare themselves, to belong to it, any otherwise than the Law directs, is at least an Evasion, if not a direct Violation of the Law, both which ought to be equally avoided.

The Town of Durham by having Eighty two of its Inhabitants employed, one Day in a Week (for we cannot suppose they will mind any other Business on those Days) for six months in military Exercises instead of their Husbandry, will sustain a Damage of L327 L.M. computing the Loss of their Labour only at half a Dollar a Day for each Person. Supposing now that all the men in the Province fit to bear Arms, which may be reasonably calculated at 14,000, should catch this military Ardor, as most Infections are catching, and according to the Tendency of this Plan, follow the Example of Durham, it would, after Durham fashion, occasion a Damage of L54,00L.M. to the Province. A pretty Tax truly for a new Country! Whatever Reason Mr. Sullivan may have to rejoice in thus leading on the People to their own Damage, I am sure the Province would have abundant Reason, not to rejoice in his Rejoicing, but to regret their own Folly; & it is well known that many are at this Day in the like Predicament on Account of some past Transactions amongst us. I hope therefore the People will judge for themselves, and avoid incurring a damage to the Province, which no doubt the Legislature had in Contemplation to prevent by limiting the Times of training the Militia to four Days in a Year."[12]

Sullivan's reply, two weeks later contains, for him, a rare bit of wit amidst the more vitriolic verbiage:

"*Mr. Printer*: In your Paper of the 17th inst. I observed a Piece signed by a Person who calls himself Monitor, full of ill–natured Reflections upon an Agreement entered into by a Number of Persons in Durham, to assemble once a Week for the Space of six Months, to instruct each other in the military Art. The feeble attempt of this scurrilous Writer, to display his Wit in the former & latter part of his nonsensical Piece, can deserve nothing but Contempt and Ridicule.

His Assertion, that a Number of Persons assembling for the Purpose of instructing each other in the Art of War, and appointing Persons to give the Words of Command, interferes with the Royal Prerogative in the Appointment of Officers, and amounts to an Evasion, if not a Violation of the Province Laws, fully demonstrates his Ignorance, both

---

12   Hammond, Otis G. Letters and Papers of Major–General John Sullivan. Volume One. Concord, N.H.   New Hampshire Historical Society,1930.pp.55–56.

of the Law and the Constitution.

The curious Calculation he makes of the Loss New Hampshire must sustain, if the same military Ardor (which he ignorantly calls an infection) should prevail throughout the Province, merits the Ridicule of all Mankind.

I am surprised, that this curious Calculation (while his Hand was in) did not inform us of the amazing Loss this Government sustains by devoting a seventh Part of the Time to religious Exercises; and endeavour to convince us, that as our Cloathing (sic) costs a large Sum, it would be best to go naked.

After which, I should be glad to know from him, if we were to lay down our Arms, and make this infamous Submission he contends for; how much Money we should be able to earn in a Day, and how much of our Earnings we should be able to keep in our Pockets.

I hope the Public will excuse my not giving a more serious and particular Answer to the Production of a dis-tempered Brain, as that might make him wise in his own Conceit, and induce this nonsensical Scribbler to think himself a Person of some Consequence.

I shall conclude with reminding him,' that a Shoe Maker never ought to go beyond his Last.'"[13]

In January, 1775, the Second Provincial Congress gathered at Exeter. Timorous at first, it refused to formally approve the raid on the fort. However, when some argued that Sullivan's motion to present a petition to Wentworth—asserting their rights and calling for an assembly Wentworth would not dissolve—was not a charge of their assembly,

---

13   Hammond, Otis G. Letters and Papers of Major-General John Sullivan. Volume One. Concord, N.H. New Hampshire Historical Society, 1930.pp.57–58.

Sullivan, the lawyer, convinced them that, since the congress was unlawful anyway, they could do anything they wanted. Furthermore, Sullivan was then allowed to draft the address they sent, which read:

"We the delegates of the several towns of this Province, assembled in Congress at Exeter, on the twenty–fifth day of January, 1775, avowing our loyalty to his Majesty, and regard for the peace and tranquility of this Province, beg leave to address your Excellency in behalf of the people, whose steady adherence to the law, and submission to legal authority, have been often acknowledged by your Excellency, and confessed by the Ministry in Great Britain.

Permit us to remind your Excellency, that, for nearly ten months past, the inhabitants of the Province, by a dissolution of their late Assembly, have been deprived of the constitutional right of having a share in their own government; and that, during the before–mentioned space of time, the whole power of government has been lodged with your Excellency and the Council, each appointed by the crown, and holding your commissions during pleasure.

We are fully sensible that the power of dissolving the Assembly of the people is, by the constitution, vested in the Crown; yet we apprehend that this, like any other prerogative, may, by an undue exercise thereof, become grievous and oppressive.

For if the prerogative can be extended to dissolve one Assembly after another, merely because the numbers differ in sentiment from his Majesty or his representative, the people cannot participate in their own legislative council unless permitted by the Crown, and must expect a dissolution of their members whenever they are represented by persons who have virtue and firmness enough to act their own judgment."[14]

In the end, they voiced support for the proceedings at Philadelphia and the association, and voted to send Sullivan and John Langdon to the Second Continental Congress.

Shortly after Sullivan and Langdon arrived at Philadelphia, in April 1775, the hostilities at Lexington and Concord brought the divisions in Congress into even sharper focus. Sullivan quickly became a major figure in John Adams's faction that felt war was inevitable—if not already begun. Moderates led by John Dickinson and James Duane felt there was still hope for reconciliation—and that actions that had or would take place were only defensive measures.

When Dickinson was able to get passed a resolution to present a "humble" petition to the King, Sullivan attacked it, to Adams's delight, "in a strain of wit, reasoning, and fluency, which…exceeded everything I had ever heard from him before."[15]

Sullivan next supported Adams's position favoring the establishment of state governments. Adams wrote:

"…it was my opinion Congress ought now to recommend to the people of every colony to…set up governments of their own under their own authority, for the people were the source of all authority and origin of all power. These were new, strange, and terrible doctrines to the greatest part of the members, but not a very small number heard them with apparent pleasure, and none more than Mr.

14   Amory, Thomas C. The Military Services and Public Life of Major-General John Sullivan. Boston, Mass. Wiggin and Lunt, 1868. pp13–14.
15   Whittemore, Charles P. A General of the Revolution. New York and London: Columbia University Press,1961.p.18

John Rutledge of South Carolina and Mr. John Sullivan of New Hampshire...Mr. Sullivan was fully agreed with me in the necessity of instituting governments, and he seconded me very handsomely in supporting the argument in Congress."[16]

Congress did come to the realization that, no matter what its ultimate course of action was to be, it had to take charge of the emerging Army. One of their tasks was to appoint its leaders. George Washington was named commander. After that, four generals and eight brigadiers were selected. Congress, perhaps feeling Sullivan's ardor was better suited for the battlefield than their chambers, selected him as the seventh brigadier.

Thus it was, Sullivan departed with Washington for Boston, prompting Adams to say he had lost an "able coadjutor".

(In time, though, Adams would also come to learn that it was not in Sullivan's character to retire from debate, even though he was heading for a battlefield. Adams "soon found the benefit of his cooperation at a distance."[17])

---

16   Hammond, Otis G. Letters and Papers of Major-General John Sullivan. Volume One. Concord, N.H.: New Hampshire Historical Society, 1930. pp9-10.
17   Hammond, Otis G. Letters and Papers of Major-General John Sullivan. Volume One. Concord, N.H.: New Hampshire Historical Society,1930.p.10.

Boston:
Chapter Four

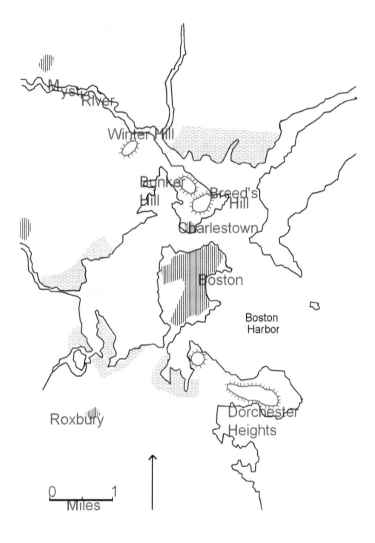

Mystic River

Winter Hill

Bunker Hill

Breed's Hill

Charlestown

Boston

Boston Harbor

Roxbury

Dorchester Heights

0   1
Miles

Siege of Boston

Unlike some, such as the more revered Thomas Jefferson, Sullivan didn't just talk about independence for the colonies, he actually fought for it. So it was, on 27June1775, that he promptly headed from Philadelphia to Boston–where the action was–arriving in Cambridge on 10July1775.

While costly to the British, the Battle of Bunker (actually, Breed's) Hill, on 17June1775, had forced the colonists to withdraw back to their original siege lines, a semicircle extending from the hills facing Charlestown Peninsula, though Roxbury, and on to Dorchester. Washington formed his forces in to three divisions. Sullivan, headquartered on Winter Hill–the post closest to the British lines–and Nathanael Greene, on Prospect Hill, were assigned brigades, under the division command of Charles Lee. To the south, Artemas Ward commanded the division in the Roxbury area. Israel Putnam commanded the third division, the "Corps–de–Reserve".

Of course, Sullivan found time during the siege to express his opinions on government and democracy, at one point writing his friend Meshech Weare :

"...no danger can arise to a state giving the people a free and full voice in their own government...for, though many states have been overturned by the rage and violence of the people, yet that spirit of rage and violence has ever been awakened in the first place by the misconduct of their rulers. Whenever this has been carried to dangerous heights, so far from being attributable to too much power being lodged in the hand of the people, it has clearly been owing to their having too small, and their rulers too extensive, a power...

I would therefore advise to such a form of government as would admit of but one object to be kept in view of the governor and the governed, namely, the good of the whole; that one interest should unite the several governing branches, and that the frequent choice of the rulers by the people should operate as a check upon their conduct, and remind them that a new election would soon honor them for their good conduct, or disgrace them for betraying the trust reposed in them..."[18]

But to literally fight for that democracy was why Sullivan had joined Washington; and Washington promptly set him to work, as Sullivan relates first in a letter to the New–Hampshire Committee of Safety on 29July1775:

> "I was preparing, when the gentleman you sent me arrived on Saturday, to take possession of the Ploughed (Plowed) Hill, near the enemy's encampment at Charleston."–(Washington both

18   Amory, Thomas C. The Military Services and Public Life of Major–General John Sullivan. Boston, Mass: Wiggin and Lunt, 1868. p.18

feared the British were about to seize the height for themselves and hoped his actions would force them in to an encounter.)–"This was done Saturday night; and, on Sunday morning, a heavy cannonading ensued, which lasted through the whole day. The floating batteries and an armed vessel attempting to come up and enfilade us as expected, a battery, which had been prepared on purpose, was opened upon them, cutting away the sloop's foresail, and making her shear off; disabling one floating battery, and sinking another. Yesterday, they sent a man–of–war to Mystick (sic) River, drew their forces from Boston, formed a long column, and prepared to come out; but, finding our readiness to receive them, declined the combat. Last evening, they began to throw bombs, but have as yet done no damage. Their cannon have been more successful, having killed three or four."[19]; and, further summarizes in a letter to John Adams, 21 Dec 1775:

"Did not the hurry of our affairs prevent, I should often write you respecting the state of our army; but it has been my fortune to be employed almost night and day. When I had Winter Hill nearly completed, I was ordered to Ploughed Hill, where for a long time I was almost day and night in fortifying. Twice have I been ordered to the Eastward, to fortify and defend Piscataway Harbour; but unfortunately was obliged to return without an opportunity of proving the works I had taken so much pains to construct. This being over, I was called upon to raise 2,000 troops from New

---

19   Ibid. , p.15

Hampshire, and bring them on the lines in ten days; this I undertook, and was happy enough to perform; otherwise the desertion of the Connecticut Troops might have proved fatal to us. I might add that 3,000 from your colony arrived at the same time to supply the defect...I have now many things to write, but must content myself with mentioning a few of them at present, and leave the residue to another opportunity. I will in the first place inform you that we have possession of almost every advantageous post around Boston, from whence we might, with great ease, burn or destroy the town, was it not we fail in a very trifling matter, namely, we have no powder to do it with. However, as we have a sufficiency for our small arms, we are not without hope to become masters of the town. Old Boreas and jack frost are now at work building a bridge over all the rivers and bays, which once completed, we take possession of the town or perish in the attempt."[20]

As Sullivan alludes to in the letter to Adams, he was one of the generals that had advised Washington, during the Fall of 1775, against attacking the British in Boston, at that time, by boat in conjunction with a land assault in Roxbury—and, instead, had recommended waiting, and attacking when winter had formed a "bridge". Little more than a week after writing Adams, Sullivan attacked Bunker Hill—while his immediate superior, General Lee, was in Rhode Island. However, whether because the ice "bridge" across a creek was still not strong enough, or because one of Sullivan's men alerted the British by accidentally discharging his firearm, the attack was aborted—and, in the process, Sullivan made enemies of Lee's friends, who accused Sullivan of trying to steal the glory of capturing

---

20   Ibid. , p.21

Bunker Hill from his superior officer.

To end the impasse, Washington had Dorchester Heights seized on 4March1776. Since General William Howe, the British Commander, realized that to attack the rebels there would be folly, Boston Harbor was now threatened by cannonade from the Heights, and therefore untenable. On 17March1776, Sullivan, using a telescope on Plowed Hill, spotted the British boarding ships. He next proceeded to Charlestown Neck for a better look at Bunker Hill—and discovered the "sentries" were "lifeless". The siege had ended; the British had evacuated the city and sailed to Halifax. Sullivan was ordered to take possession of Charlestown, while Israel Putnam occupied Boston. On 18March1776, Sullivan was one of the party that escorted Commander–in–Chief Washington in to Boston.

CANADA
Chapter Five

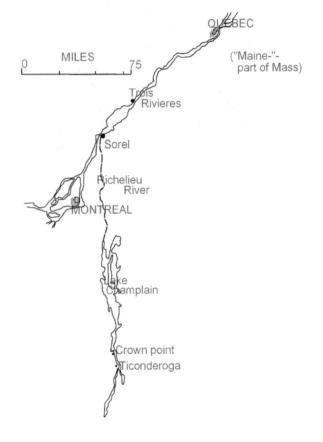

QUEBEC

MILES

0   75

("Maine-"-
part of Mass)

Trois
Rivieres

Sorel

Richelieu
River

MONTREAL

Lake
Champlain

Crown point
Ticonderoga

CHAPTER **Five**

Canada

It wasn't long before Washington had another task for the energetic Sullivan; but, first, Sullivan had to deal with the backbiting that always seemed to follow his successes like a shadow.

First, the New Hampshire legislature – feeling it was their prerogative–criticized Sullivan for appointing officers, which Sullivan had done of necessity to get as many New Hampshire men to re–enlist as possible, at a time when the militia was threatening to leave. One can't blame Sullivan–knowing he was soon off to action again–for irately responding: " then those persons will ... have no more fear of the Destruction of their Liberties from a person who has Spent more money undergone more Fatigue and oftener Risqued (sic) his Life than any other person in your Province & all this to Secure that Freedom which those Gentleman would perswade (sic) the world I am Endeavouring (sic) to Destroy ".[21]

21   Whittemore, Charles P. A General of the Revolution New York and London: Columbia University Press, 1961. p.25

Other complaints dealt with whether he had or had not been improperly reimbursed for expenses—or even should be reimbursed, as some in the legislature requested. Sullivan wrote to the New Hampshire General Assembly: " I sensibly feel my Obligation to those Gentlemen who actuated by motives of Justice and Humanity made the motion without my knowledge or Consent, but at the Same time must beg leave to assure them that the loss of Interest and fatigues of War are what I expect nothing in Return for except seeing My Country freed from Slavery and those worthy Gentlemen and their posterity Enjoying the Sweets of peace and freedom ". [22]

Meanwhile, as the Siege of Boston was ending, bad news was arriving from Canada. On 31Jan1775, General Richard Montgomery, coming from Montreal, which he had captured in November, linked up with an expeditionary force that Benedict Arnold—the victor at Fort Ticonderoga in May—had brought up through Maine from Boston, in order to jointly attack Quebec City. The British, reinforced with troops from England under Burgoyne, soundly defeated the Colonial forces, and forced their retreat back towards Montreal, in the process killing Montgomery, wounding Arnold, and taking many prisoners. The remaining Colonists were further prostrated by smallpox and the rigors of the harsh Canadian winter. Simply put, things were in a mess in Canada—and, as would be repeated often in the years ahead, Sullivan was the one Washington dispatched to rectify a difficult situation—in this case to extricate the northern army. In May 1775, Sullivan was sent from New York, up the Hudson, with approximately 3,000 men. Arriving in early June, he found chaos, with troops

22   Ibid

deserting—and those remaining widely dispersed and short of supplies.

However, even though in this instance discretion would have been the better part of valor, it was not Sullivan's nature to quit without a fight—and to want Washington and Congress to know it. When he heard from Brigadier General Thompson—who had replaced Montgomery and Arnold in command—that the British had advanced to Trois Rivieres , Sullivan hurried to join Thompson at Sorel, and then to send him to attack what was thought to be 300 (as of the last intelligence report) British regulars at Trois Rivieres. For disputed reasons, Thompson failed to surprise the enemy, now also well reinforced beyond 300; and the British Commander, General Guy Carleton, drove the Revolutionaries back on 11June—but failed to aggressively pursue the retreat (which subsequently caused London to transfer command of the British in the North to Burgoyne). (Sullivan—phobe historians malign the attack on Trois—Rivieres ; but, one can wonder if it was part of the reason Carleton hesitated. If so, Carleton would not be the first—or last—commander to over—estimate an enemy's strength just because they attacked, and to be satisfied with just beating off the attack.) Though Sullivan was still reluctant to flee—and, in his frustration, blemishing his record by blaming the failure of the attack on those under him for a failure of will—he finally acceded to a Council of War, held the night of 13 June, and ordered retreat.

Considering the wretched condition of the army, Sullivan carried out a surprisingly orderly and efficient retreat, as he proudly wrote John Hancock upon reaching Crown Point the night of 1July1776.

Earlier, Sullivan had written a letter to Washington hint-ing he would like the Canadian command. This Washington sent on to Congress 17 June 1776, along with the opinion Sullivan was "active, spirited, and Zealously (sic) attached to the Cause (sic), but also had a little tincture of vanity…an over desire of being popular, which now and then leads him into some embarrassments."[23] However, while saying it was because they preferred a more experienced man–but probably because Sullivan was not at all "popular" with many in Congress–Horatio Gates was chosen by Congress to supersede him.

Sullivan was so angered by this concluded lack of faith in him that he returned to Philadelphia, the end of July, and offered his resignation. This resignation many of his "arm–chair warrior " enemies, led by Thomas Jefferson, were only too glad to accept. His friends, though, urged Sullivan to reconsider–with John Hancock providing the explanation that, in the end, was acceptable enough for Sullivan to allow him to tactfully reconsider.

Fortunately for "the Cause", Sullivan withdrew his resignation, on 29 July 1776; and soon he was on his way to perform yet another mission for General Washington.

---

23   Whittemore, Charles P. A General of the Revolution. New York and London: Columbia University Press, 1961. p.30

LONG ISLAND

Chapter Six

0 1 2 3 4
Miles

New
Jersey

East
River

New
York

Brooklyn

New York Bay

LONG ISLAND

Gowanus
Road

Bedford
Road

Flatbush
Road

Jamaica
Pass

Staten
Island

Gravesend

CHAPTER **Six**

Long Island and Capture

Initially, in 1776, the British launched an offensive in the Carolinas, believing that would bolster southern loyalists. However, on 28June1776, Major General Sir Henry Clinton's attempt to seize Charleston, South Carolina was repulsed; and the British then turned their attention to New York. New York was considered by Major General Sir William Howe to be of more strategic importance than Charleston, and he wished to capture New York intact for use as winter quarters for his troops.

General Washington, also aware of the importance of New York, concentrated his army around it, and prepared for its defense.

A key part of the defense was fortifying the Brooklyn Heights on the western end of Long Island, not only because they dominated the East River, but because Washington hoped the British would try to take it by frontal assault as they had—with disastrous losses —at Bunker(Breed's) Hill. Nathanael Greene, whom Washington considered his most trustworthy general, was initially placed in command at this location; but, on 20Aug1776, Greene, "dangerously ill", had to be relieved. To replace Greene, Washington chose Sullivan, recently promoted to Major General.

Sullivan's promotion, despite the enmity of many, once again demonstrated that Washington, actually at the scene of action, had confidence in Sullivan. But Washington also knew impulsiveness was a short–coming of Sullivan's; so Washington, fearing Sullivan might attack the British, rather than let them make the first move, then sent "Old Put" (Israel Putnam) to supervise Sullivan, causing an ambiguity of command.

As things turned out, the British, who landed an invasion force south of the American Long Island position, on 22August1776, did not take Washington's bait and attack head on. Instead, Howe would use a plan to outflank the rebel army devised by Henry Clinton, a strategist who knew well how to use a map (" 'Look at the map,' he would proclaim."[24]).

There were three main roads approaching the American positions from the south: Gowanus on the Colonist's far right, nearest the narrows; Flatbush Road, the presumed British route, in the center; and Bedford Road off to the left. After looking things over with his commanders, on 26August1776, Washington approved a plan that placed Lord Stirling in command of the right, Sullivan in command of the center at Flatbush Pass, and Colonel Miles on the left, to watch for movement from the direction of Bedford Road–all three of them under the direction of General Putnam, stationed on Brooklyn Heights. At the last minute,

---

24 McCullough, David 1776 New York: Simon & Schuster,2005. p.165

presumably also with Washington's approval, Sullivan posted a mounted patrol of five young militia officers to watch the little–used Jamaica Pass, through the wooded heights, three miles to the east of the American lines. They were to serve only as an "early warning system", since a permanent post there could be easily cut off from the American lines, the only point of retreat.

At the same time Washington was giving his commanders their assignments, Howe sent for Clinton, and told him to attack according to his plan that night. Thus, at nightfall, leaving their campfires burning, Clinton quietly led the major attacking force northeast out of their encampment at Gravesend. By two AM they had reached Howard's Tavern, at the entrance to the Jamaica Pass, which was unguarded.

A group of British officers was then sent ahead to scout the pass. Shortly after leaving the tavern, they encountered the Americans on patrol. In the darkness, supposing the approaching figures to be more of their own, the Americans casually joined them. Without a shot being fired, the Americans were captured–and any chance Washington's soldiers at Brooklyn had of being fore–warned, and of avoiding their up–coming debacle, disappeared.

Clinton and the advance units immediately started through the narrow pass, and as dawn broke, on 27August1776, they were on the road, situated on the north side of the ridge, that ran east to west from Jamaica towards Bedford. It took another two hours for Howe, with the remainder of the column, plus supporting artillery and wagons, to get through and join the others, who were resting by the road. So far, everything had gone according to Clinton's plan; and the British were in position to attack when, also right on schedule, two cannon blasts signaled that two frontal diversionary attacks on the Americans were under way—a British one, led by General Grant along the Gowanus Road against the American right; and one by Hessians, under General von Heister, against the center, up the Bedford Road towards Flatbush Pass. The Americans went for the bait, fought ardently, and felt they were holding their own against British regulars—until shots were heard coming from the direction of Bedford, in their rear, and they realized they were surrounded.

Sullivan immediately began to re-adjust his troops to counter the sudden deterioration in their situation. In his book, "1776", David McCullough recounts Sullivan's actions at this time; and, since it is a rare instance of an established historian speaking of Sullivan in a positive way, it is worth repeating it verbatim:

"Leaving his advance guard posted along the ridge to do what they could to hold off the Hessians, Sullivan pulled back his main force and swung around to face the oncoming British ranks. And although vastly outnumbered, the Americans returned the British fire with murderous effect. Officers on both sides feared their men would be cut to pieces, and officers and soldiers on both sides often had no idea what was happening. Nor was it the Americans only who, when faced with annihilation, ran for their lives.....

In the turmoil and confusion, Sullivan struggled to hold control and keep his men from panicking. Their situation was desperate; retreat was the only alternative, and in stages of 'fight and flight', he lead them as rapidly as possible in the direction of the Brooklyn lines...

Those left to hold the ridge had by now been overrun by the Hessians. At the same time, the whole left side of the American line collapsed. Thousands of men were on the run, hundreds were captured. Sullivan held back, in an effort to see as many as possible to safety, and amazingly most of the men succeeded in reaching the Brooklyn lines.

Sullivan, however, was captured. An American soldier named Lewis Morris, who himself barely escaped, wrote of Sullivan in a letter home. 'The last I heard of him, he was in a cornfield close by our lines, with a pistol in each hand, and the enemy had formed a line each side of him, and he was going directly between them...' "[25]

As was Patton in WW2, Sullivan was the general the enemy came to fear most–a soldier's highest compliment–and this was evidenced by what his delighted captors stated of Sullivan at the time. "Sullivan was bred to the law, and is said to be one of their best officers", wrote a British officer in his diary.[26]"A man of genius", stated a German one.[27]

General William Howe, Commander–in–Chief of the British land forces, transferred Sullivan, and the also captured Lord Stirling, to the ship of Admiral Lord Richard Howe, Commander of the North American Station–and William's older brother. Both brothers were anxious to end the conflict in a peaceful way; and in the years prior to the Revolution Lord Richard , as a member of Parliament, had both voted against coercive measures towards the colonies and consulted with Benjamin Franklin–then in England–in an attempt to work out compromise peace proposals. Lord Richard felt his orders allowed him and his brother to settle

25   McCullough, David. 1776. New York: Simon & Schuster, 2005. pp.173–174
26   Whittemore, Charles P. A General of the Revolution. New York and London: Columbia University Press, 1961.p.40
27   Ibid

the dispute between England and America, so it was only to be expected he saw Sullivan's capture as a way to set up a peace conference with representatives from the colonies. One can also understand why Sullivan, who only hours before had seen his countrymen bayoneted by overwhelming numbers of Hessians and Highlanders, might also be desirous for the bloodshed to come to an end—even though his actions in this regard would draw ire from those who followed the war from afar.

On 30August1776, Sullivan was paroled; and on September 2nd, with Washington's permission, he arrived in Philadelphia. On 3September, as Jefferson fled town to over–see the building of Monticello, Sullivan presented to Congress Lord Howe's request for a conference. As he did so, John Adams, who was safely ensconced in Philadelphia while Sullivan was facing the enemy with a brace of pistols and directing his men to safety, waspishly whispered to Benjamin Rush " how much better it would have been had a musket ball at Long Island gone through Sullivan's head."[28]

Despite Adams's objections to the conference–he felt Lord Howe was trying to trick them in to giving up their quest for independence– Congress not only voted to send a committee to meet with Lord Howe, they chose Adams, along with Benjamin Franklin and Edward Rutledge, for the mission. Adams consented to go–to make sure, he wrote, "as little evil might come of it, as possible".[29]

Lord Howe met with the American delegation on Staten Island, the 11th of September, 1776. He began by express-

28   McCullough, David. <u>John Adams</u>. New York: Simon & Schuster, 2001.p.154
29   Ibid

ing his great affection for America, averring, "If America should fail, I should feel and lament it like the loss of a brother."[30]Franklin replied, "My lord, we will do our utmost endeavors to save your Lordship that mortification."[31] While this bit of banter, between two former friends, set the tone for a civil conclave, any chance of reconciliation was doomed from the beginning, because of Lord Howe's insistence that the Declaration of Independence be rescinded before negotiations could proceed further–since the Americans were equally determined not to give up their goal of independence.

One of Howe's staff summarized the day: "They met, they talked, they parted, and now nothing remains but to fight it out..."[32]However, while nothing was accomplished, rather than harming the American cause, as Adams had feared, their having agreed to meet proved to be beneficial to the Americans in two ways.

Those Americans favoring independence rejoiced upon hearing that nothing had resulted from this face to face meeting with British authority; and, psychologically, this first test of the Declaration of Independence more firmly united the country.

From a military standpoint, the authors of "The West Point Atlas of American Wars" opined that "[Major General] Howe lost two weeks in fruitless peace negotiations with a Congressional committee."[33] Under miraculous circumstances, on the night of 29–30August1776, the Americans had evacuated Brooklyn and arrived in New York, without

30   Ibid p.157
31   Ibid
32   Ibid p.158
33   Esposito, Vincent J. The West Point Atlas of American Wars. New York: Frederick A. Praeger, 1959. p.Map 5

a loss of life. While the negotiations were being set up and held, William Howe suspended operations—even though the late–summer days that slipped by would have been perfect for attack—again letting the Americans survive to fight another day.

Upon conclusion of the peace proceedings, Sullivan and Lord Stirling were exchanged—Sullivan for British General Richard Prescott. (Prescott was subsequently re–captured in a raid on his quarters in Rhode Island. Otherwise he might have faced Sullivan in the 1778 Battle of Rhode Island.)

Sullivan rejoined Washington the end of September, once again arriving to find the American forces in a shameful and chaotic condition. Also upon conclusion of the peace negotiations, the British had promptly returned to the offensive. On 15Sept1776 they had launched an amphibious assault upon Manhattan Island, which caused the already dispirited Americans to flee New York in panic. But, in the days to come, Sullivan would again prove to be one American who was not only "zealous", but competent.

NEW JERSEY :

Chapter Seven

New Jersey: Trenton and Princeton

With a series of flanking attacks, initially amphibious, General Howe drove the Americans first from New York, and then off Manhattan Island entirely; so that by the end of November 1776, Washington was withdrawing the demoralized rebels, weakened by desertions, southwards across New Jersey towards the Delaware River.

General Greene had joined forces with Washington at Hackensack. With Cornwallis close on their heels, they reached the Delaware at Trenton; and, on 7December1776, crossed the river into Pennsylvania, first destroying all boats they were not using. Despite the dire circumstances, it had been an orderly retreat, with few casualties; and those Americans who had persevered meant Washington still had an army. He now awaited General Charles Lee, with the remainder of the American forces, to join him.

Sullivan had been assigned to serve under Lee's command. However, Lee was not responding to Washington's request to join him with the same alacrity his next–in–command would eventually demonstrate; and, although Washington eagerly awaited his arrival, Lee was still tarrying in northern New Jersey. Not only that, but, on the night of 12December1776, Lee left his troops under Sullivan's command, and then rode three miles away, to spend a comfortable night at Widow White's tavern, in Basking Ridge. While still lounging in his dressing gown the next morning–Friday the 13th–Lee was surrounded and captured by a party of British cavalry, tipped–off by a local Loyalist.

"Sullivan heard the news that morning when Lee's aide, Major William Bradford, rode up to tell of the general's capture. Upon hearing the report, 'Sullivan rode through the line giving orders, to show that we still had a commander left , and did not appear to regret the loss of Lee.' Once General Sullivan realized that he had no chance of rescuing his superior, he did not hesitate to move; he pressed his men toward the Delaware and junction with Washington."[34] Thus, on 20 December, in the midst of a snowstorm, Sullivan–no "summer soldier" in any sense of the term–led Lee's troops in to Washington's camp, above Trenton Falls, arriving in one quarter of the time Lee had planned.

Although the British were exultant about the capture of Lee—since, as a British soldier and gentleman, they considered him not only superior to raw provincials, but also a traitor—events would show Sullivan replacing Lee was one of the reasons Friday the 13th turned out to be a lucky day for the Americans. The other was General William Howe

34   Whittemore, Charles P. A General of the Revolution. New York and London : Columbia University Press, 1961. p.44

deciding, on that day, to suspend military operations until spring, and to take his army in to winter quarters in northern New Jersey and New York City, leaving a string of outposts to guard the ground gained in New Jersey.

Following Long Island, Washington had assiduously avoided any general or risky action. However, with the spirits of the Continentals at a miserable low, he now felt compelled to attempt a surprise attack, and hope that, with luck, it would succeed; and, consequently, that would raise the morale of the Americans. It was to be against the closest concentration of the foe, just across the Delaware River, in Trenton, New Jersey.   Located there was a force of Hessians, under the command of Colonel Johann Rall, an able, veteran soldier, who had bravely led the successful Hessian assaults that had driven the Americans from White Plains and Fort Washington, starting them on their retreat across New Jersey. Also, contrary to myth, with Teutonic thoroughness, Rall, even during Christmas time, was constantly on guard, with regular outposts outside of town and, at night, a company on the alert with loaded muskets. However, the "good luck" that would give Washington his success would prove to be the weather—and a mix–up in communications along the British force chain–of–command, which led to confusion over warnings of the impending attack.

Washington's plan called for the attack to begin with a crossing of the Delaware at Midnight, December 25–Christmas night–then marching through that night, so as to arrive at Trenton just before dawn.(Originally, besides what would be the main crossing at McConkey's Ferry, nine miles upstream from Trenton, there were to be two other crossings–one directly across from Trenton and one downstream—but the latter two were called off at the last moment, because of the treacherous conditions caused by ice in the river.)

Christmas night, as the main force of Continentals started the crossing, the weather conditions were horrific—though that would prove to be the proverbial "blessing in disguise"—with a "noreaster" howling, and ice chunks choking the river. But, as they had done before, and would do again, Colonel John Glover and his tough Massachusetts fishermen successfully transported the Americans. On the other side, behind schedule, but determined to continue with the attack, Washington led his 2,400 men south five miles to the crossroads at Birmingham, where he divided his army. Greene, whom Washington would accompany, would lead his detachment along the upper—the inland—Pennington Road. Sullivan was separately assigned to lead his force along the lower River Road. (Either way, the distance to Trenton was about four miles.) So, "the stage was set": as the Congress that so maligned Sullivan fled from Philadelphia to Baltimore, Sullivan was once again to prove himself to be a brave and tireless fighter—and perhaps Washington's best field commander.

Despite having to march under the most adverse of conditions, within minutes of each other, at about 8AM, the two columns commenced to attack Trenton simultaneously—Greene's from the north, and Sullivan's from the south. Knox's artillery with Greene opened fire from the head of King and Queen Streets; and, as the Hessians fled from that, they encountered Sullivan's men coming at them with fixed bayonets, their guns too soaked to fire. Colonel Rall had quickly entered the fray on horseback. Rall first ordered a charge; but, as his men fell all around him, he then had them retreat to an orchard southeast of town, where he too was mortally wounded. At this point, after only forty–five minutes of battle, the Hessians surrendered. At the cost of only four battle–wounded —though two had frozen to death during the night march–the Americans had killed twenty–one Hessians, wounded 90, captured 900, and caused another 500 to flee for their lives.

Then, after all this, as incredible as it seems, they marched back the nine miles and re–crossed the Delaware, taking their 900 prisoners and six pieces of captured artillery with them.

Buoyed by success–and anxious to continue the impetus it provided, in order to keep his army going–Washington quickly decided to go after the enemy again. On 29December1776, Washington, Greene, and Sullivan and their troops–and artilleryman Knox with 40 cannon and their horses–again crossed the Delaware and marched to Trenton, arriving 30 December.

The following day, the last day of 1776, was a crucial one, for at that time the enlistments of many of the veteran Continentals expired. As he had also done outside of Boston, Sullivan once again, "behind the scenes", helped Washington–and the cause–by successfully prevailing on his troops to "tarry six weeks after the first day of January, which in my opinion went far towards saving America"[35].

In response to Washington's Christmas coup de main, General Howe had sent Cornwallis, with a reinforced legion, into New Jersey to crush the rebels, once and for all. Cornwallis and his army reached Princeton on 1January1777. On the second, he left a detachment in Princeton

---

35   Amory, Thomas C. The Military Services and Public Life of Major–General John Sullivan. Boston, Mass.: Wiggin and Lunt, 1868. p.52

and marched with the main part of his force (5,500 men) to Trenton, 10 miles away. Muddy roads and American harassment, directed by Sullivan, slowed the British column, so that Cornwallis did not arrive at Trenton until 4PM, just as winter darkness also came. Rather than risk a night attack, with troops exhausted from the day's difficult march, Cornwallis decided to wait until morning "to bag the fox".

During the early hours of 3January1777, leaving campfires burning and making the noises of an army settling in for the night, Washington and some 5,500 men, horses, and cannon quietly set out for Princeton on a wide sweep—first to the east, and then north, along little–known back roads. In this manner, Washington planned to turn the flank of the British and attack their rear guard—entrenched only along the main Post Road to Trenton—via a Princeton back road.

Approaching Princeton at sunrise, 3January, Washington again sent Greene's force to the left—to cut off the bridge where the Post Road crosses Stony Brook, preventing retreat from Princeton and reinforcement from Trenton—and Sullivan's to the right, to continue along the Back Road in to Princeton. As battle began, the British here were even more astonished to see so many Americans attacking them than the Hessians had been at Trenton.

In fighting as bloody as any of the war, the Americans drove the redcoats from the fields and orchards south of Princeton. Most of the British—along with their Commander at Princeton, Colonel Charles Mawhood—fled south towards the main force in Trenton. A smaller contingent fled into the college yard. There, some surrendered to Sullivan, while others barricaded themselves inside Nassau Hall—only to also quickly surrender upon coming under the fire of American cannons.

Again flush with victory, Washington—and, one might also assume, Sullivan—now wanted to push on to Brunswick, and capture enemy supplies and their pay chest stored there; but the cooler heads of Greene and Knox convinced Washington not to aim at too much and lose all —and it was decided not to pursue further action at this time. Instead, Washington led his exhausted army in to the security of the woods around Morristown, New Jersey, to spend the remainder of the winter.

" *THE SPIRIT OF 1776"* ENDS.....

ON TO 1777

STATEN
ISLAND:

Chapter
Eight

New Jersey

3 MILES

NJ

NEW YORK
BAY

DECKER'S
FERRY

ARTHUR
KILL

STATEN
ISLAND

Long
Island

FRESH KILL
BLAZING
STAR

AMBOY

RARITAN
BAY

CHAPTER **Eight**

Staten Island and Controversy

While 1776 ended well for Sullivan, 1777 had an inauspicious beginning.

Setting the tone, a chronic gastro–intestinal illness, that was to plague him throughout life, was in a particularly painful phase. Since another symptom was bleeding, the presumed diagnosis of peptic ulcer is probably correct, especially considering Sullivan's temperament–and fits with the admonition of his doctor " to avoid the free use of spirits".

Anyway, it certainly couldn't have been soothing for his ulcer when he heard, at this time, that Washington had put General Arthur St. Clair in command at Ticonderoga, a posting Sullivan wished for himself. Naturally enough, Sullivan shot off an irate letter to Washington, beginning:

"...Dear Genl ...I have been Informed that Genl St Clair is to take the Command at Ticonderoga the Ensueing (sic) Campaign. Though I never wish to Complain I can't help the Disagreeable feeling So Common to mankind when they find themselves Slighted & Neglected—when I had Completed the Disagreeable retreat from Canada I was Superseaded (sic) with Circumstances of Indignity Since which & before Every Major General Except myself have had the Honor of Commanding posts Seperated (sic) from the main Army..."[36]—whom Sullivan then enumerates, in detail. He ends by "claiming it as my right" that the next separate post be entrusted to his care.

Washington promptly and pithily replied:

"Do not, my dear General Sullivan, torment yourself any longer with imaginary slights, and involve others in the perplexities you feel on that score. No other officer of rank in the whole army has so often conceived himself neglected, slighted, and ill treated as you have done, and none I am sure has had less cause than yourself to entertain such ideas...", which Washington then expounds upon—then ends by frankly informing Sullivan, "keeping in mind, at the same time, that if distant armies are to be formed there are several gentlemen before you in point of rank who have a right to claim a reference."[37]

(As things turned out, Sullivan was probably lucky he did not receive the Ticonderoga command. British forces, moving south from Canada under General Burgoyne, forced St. Clair to evacuate Ticonderoga on 6July1777; and, though Sullivan may have thought otherwise, he would probably have fared no better than St. Clair, under the circumstances.)

Sullivan, though, did acknowledge Washington's re-

---

36 Hammond, Otis G. Letters and Papers of Major-General John Sullivan I. Concord, N.H. New Hampshire Historical Society, 1930. pp.326–327.
37 Ibid pp.328–329

buke–by returning from sick leave to his post in northern New Jersey. But, it wasn't long before he was again writing to not only Washington, but also to John Hancock, about a personal matter, albeit in this case his cause was more worthy – and concerned not himself, but his younger brother, Captain Ebenezer Sullivan.

Ebenezer had been part of the garrison at Fort Cedars, near Montreal, that had surrendered to a larger British force on 16May1776. Major Isaac Butterfield, the American commander, and the British commander, Captain George Foster, agreed to a cartel wherein the British would acquire the fort, without a fight, in exchange for the British protecting the Americans from their atrocity–committing Iroquois Indian allies. As part of this agreement, so General Sullivan wrote Hancock, Ebenezer " voluntarily became a hostage for the redemption of a number of our Troops & during his stay with the Enemy suffered incredible Insults and hardships, he was sent home on his promise to remain a true prisoner & return again when called for...Upon his arrival here...he can neither joyn (sic) the Army, or with any propriety enter upon any other business, as he knows not the hour he will be called for...", and Sullivan ends with the not un–reasonable request ," I hope Congress will contrive some ways of restoring him to the Community, & of reimbursing him for the losses of Money & other Articles which he has sustained...& to continue his pay while he remains in his present Situation. And also to reserve for him that rank in the Army which he might have had if not held as Hostage for the fulfillment of the Articles of Capitulation".[38]

(Whether because of his surname or not, Captain

---

38   Ibid pp.420–422

Sullivan was not assisted by the members of Congress–who had never experienced being tied to a stake, expecting to be burned alive. Captain Sullivan was finally exchanged in 1778.)

Still another imbroglio involved Sullivan, this time affecting him only indirectly. An acquaintance of Sullivan's from New Hampshire, Peter Livius, wrote him anonymously from Montreal, on 2June1777, urging him to "retrace his steps" and come over to the British side. However, the proposal never reached Sullivan, because Philip Schuyler caught the courier en route. Since it seemed the British thought Sullivan had been given the command at Ticonderoga, once Sullivan heard of the letter, through Washington, he agreed "to play along", if it would help Washington. However, this intriguing plot came to naught. Schuyler had already sent a reply, as if it were from Sullivan–and nothing further was heard from Canada.

Perhaps incited by all these frustrations, by the time the summer of 1777 arrived Sullivan was craving action; and in his theater of operations there was a vexation that he felt called for retaliation: British troops and Tory loyalists on Staten Island, about 20 miles south–east of his base at Hanover, New Jersey, were launching raids along the Jersey shore to harass inhabitants and capture cattle.

On 21August1777, Sullivan marched his troops south–east out of their encampment. (In order to mask his objective from Loyalists that would alert Staten Island, he had put out word that he had been ordered to Philadelphia.) During the night march, Sullivan divided his forces, planning to disembark on Staten Island at two different crossing points. Before daylight, on the 22nd, his well coordinated, two–pronged attack began as planned.

Crossing from the Jersey side of the Blazing Star Ferry, but then landing up the Fresh Kill , Colonel Ogden with two regiments surprised the British stationed at the Staten Island quay by attacking them from behind – and quickly put an end to their opposition. Along with the British commander there–Colonel Lawrence–Ogden captured 100 soldiers, a large quantity of stores, and a sloop.

Sullivan, with Generals Smallwood and DeBorres and their men, landed at the north end of the island, near Decker's Ferry. Here, too, there was initial success, with Smallwood's division routing the British provincials, located at Decker's Ferry.

However, there then began a series of those un–anticipated misfortunes of war one can never plan for.

Whether by accident or design, Americans coming from the north, who were to cut off the retreat of the British, were misled by their guide to the front, rather than to the rear, of the enemy, thus enabling the British to escape being surrounded.

Meanwhile, the boatmen bringing the boats from the northern landing site down the Arthur Kill to the Blazing Star Ferry – where all the Americans were to re–cross to New Jersey–spotted the sloop captured by Ogden sailing towards them. Supposing it to be a British tender attacking them, they turned away. Other boatmen from the Jersey shore were frightened off by the red–coated assemblage of Ogden's prisoners. Consequently, there were, then, only three boats at the Blazing Star to evacuate the Americans.

Sullivan realized he had better start getting his now exhausted troops back to New Jersey as quickly as possible–which he immediately began doing. However, once most of the Americans had crossed, the British marched out of hiding to attack the American rear guard, of about 100 men.

Though now out–numbered, the remaining Americans put up a stiff resistance–fighting until their ammunition was totally expended. While battle raged on Staten Island, Sullivan, on the Jersey shore, was attempting to get boats to return for his troops, by providing a covering fire, "...but the Boatmen were so frightened by their [British] Field pieces that they would not cross Though I ordered our people from this shore to fire upon them to Drive them over they rowed out in the middle of the Sound & could not be prevailed upon to come to one side or the other. The officers Seeing this Thought proper to Surrender with about forty men. The Rest made their Escape Some by Swimming & others by going to Amboy where I Sent to provide a Boat for them." (sic)[39]

The following day, an exchange of prisoners was arranged. British casualties were greater than American. Also, the British suffered "the Loss of their vessels Stores Baggage Arms tents &c and also A Large Quantity of Hay they had Collected which we Destroyed" (sic). So, while the raid did not turn out to be the brilliant success it almost was, neither was it a significant defeat for the Americans. Of course Sullivan's enemies–and he now had gained more as a result of insinuating remarks he had made about St. Clair having to surrender Ticonderoga–claimed that it was. In answer to these complaints he demanded, and secured, a court of inquiry, which unanimously reported on 12Oct1777:

"That the expedition against the enemy on Staten Island was eligible, and promised great advantage to the

---

39   Ibid p.441

cause of America; that it was well concerted and the orders for the execution proper; and would have succeeded, with reputation to the general and his troops, had it not in some measure been rendered abortive by accidents which were out of the power of the general to foresee or prevent " and that " General Sullivan's conduct in planning and executing the expedition was such that, in the opinion of this court, he deserves the approbation of the country and not its censure."[40]

As it happened, even before this report came out Sullivan had once again fought on the battlefield—and was once again involved in a war of words with his own countrymen. Ironically, on the very day of Sullivan's Staten Island raid, Washington had indeed written an order to Sullivan to join him near Philadelphia.

---

40   Ibid pp.16–17

BRANDYWINE & GERMANTOWN

Chapters 9 & 10

Valley Forge

Schuylkill River

Jefferis's Fd

PA

Germantown Rds Limekiln

Mt Airy
Chew Hs
Mt Sq
German-town

B r a n
Buffington's Fd
Wistar's Fds
Jones's
Osborne's Hill
Birmingham Hts

Trimble's Fd

Howe/ Cornwallis Route

C r e e k

Brinton's Fd

Philadelphia

Kennett Square

× Chad's Fd

Chester

Delaware River

NJ

Wilmington

DEL

0   5   10
Miles

MD

Head of Elk

CHAPTER Nine

Brandywine and Its Aftermath

That July (1777) General Sir William Howe had embarked from New York, with 13,000 British and 5,000 Hessian troops—to sail south, and then into the Chesapeake Bay. Washington correctly assumed Philadelphia was Howe's objective–and that steps must be taken to defend the capital of the fledgling United States. To help him accomplish that crucial task, he once again turned to Sullivan; and, on 22August, he ordered Sullivan to join his army west of Philadelphia.

On 24August, Howe landed near Head of Elk, Maryland, and started advancing slowly northward. Washington, planning to make his stand behind Brandywine Creek, about twenty miles below Philadelphia, marched south. On 9September, Howe's army arrived at Kennett Square, Pennsylvania, six miles west of the Chad's Ford crossing of Brandywine Creek. Facing him here now, from the other side of Brandywine Creek, was Washington, with 11,000 American soldiers.

Washington had established his headquarters on the high ground just east of Chad's Ford. Nathaniel Greene was in command of the left wing and the reserve, also at Chad's Ferry. Sullivan was to command the right wing. When he reported to Washington, on 10September1777, he was instructed by Washington to station himself with the main body of his troops at Brinton's Ford—and to also deploy elements to cover the Jones's, Wistar's, and Buffington's Fords above. Sullivan had just arrived, and he had not yet had the opportunity to reconnoiter the ground for himself. However, after Long Island, he was quite mindful of Howe's propensity to use flanking attacks; and he asked Washington and his staff if there were any fords above Buffington's. Because the local families that favored the American cause had fled, much of the information about the area that Washington had gleaned was inaccurate, including being told the next ford upstream from Buffington's was 12 miles away—and that the roads to it were almost inaccessible; this is what Washington then told Sullivan. However, as a precaution against surprise, Washington did send out Colonels Ross and Bland and Major Spear with patrols of mounted scouts.

Howe, having more accurate information about other fords, thanks to local Tories, was indeed about to execute a flanking maneuver—and around Sullivan, again, as it turned out. While Hessian General Wilhelm von Knyphausen and his 5,000 Hessians would feint an attack on Chad's Ford to preoccupy Washington, General Charles Cornwallis with the rest of the army would make a wide sweep to the left of the Americans. They would march north along the Great Valley Road, which paralleled Brandywine Creek, cross its west branch at Trimble's Ford and its east branch at Jefferis's Ford, and then turn south to attack the American right wing from behind. Once Knyphausen heard the sound of Cornwallis's guns, he was to launch a real attack across Chad's Ford and link up with Cornwallis.

At 4AM the morning of 11 September 1777, Cornwallis's column, with Howe accompanying Cornwallis, began its march north towards the branches of the Brandywine. At 8AM, Knyphausen's force started east towards the Brandywine. Easily driving off an advance party of Americans on the west side of the creek, by 10AM the Hessians had gained the high ground opposite Greene; and from here they started a cannonade—and a movement of troops as if they were about to attack. However, the demonstration failed to fool Washington, who now decided Howe had indeed divided his forces—and that the bulk was probably now marching around his right flank.

About 11AM, a dispatch arrived from Ross's scouting party that said Howe, with a large body of the enemy, was moving up the Great Valley Road. This confirmed Washington's belief that Howe had divided his forces—and that he could now attack the British in detail. He would have his entire army cross the Brandywine, defeat Knyphausen's section, then re–cross in time to face Howe coming at his rear–not only a fool–hardy plan, but one based on his erroneous belief that Howe's group had a twelve mile march before they could cross to the east side of the Brandywine. When, after this decision had been made, Sullivan's aide, Major John Eustace, rode up to report he, too, had seen British movements indicating they were intending to turn the right flank, both Washington and Henry Knox laughed—

presumably at the thought they were going to make Howe pay for his actions this time.

But Greene's advance troops were barely across the creek when another dispatch from Sullivan arrived at Washington's headquarters: A Major Spear, of the Pennsylvania militia and familiar with the area, had scouted the terrain between the two branches above Buffington's Ford and had seen nothing of the enemy. This was counter to the belief of both Sullivan and Washington that the enemy was attempting a flanking march—and was actually old intelligence, since Spear had done his reconnaissance early in the morning—but Washington accepted it, which may have actually been providential. Now, fearing the march north was a feint—and that the entire British force was across from Chad's Ford—Washington ordered Greene's advance troops withdrawn, and then canceled the orders for the entire army to cross the creek. (One can well imagine how much more disastrous the day would have been for the Americans if they had been on the west side of the Brandywine when Howe hit their rear!)

At this point, Washington essentially decided to wait it out. When he had ordered Greene's frontal attack, he had also sent a contingent under Adam Stephen and Thomas Stirling to the region south of Osborne Hill, where he expected, at that time, Howe would emerge; so, he must have felt he had all approaches covered. Although many historians fault Washington for thus handing over the initiative to the enemy—and even, some said, acting "as if in a daze"—it would seem, under the circumstances, he had little other choice.

Anyway, Washington didn't have long to wait. Shortly

after 2PM another message arrived from Sullivan :

"*Dear General* Col Bland "–whom Washington had
sent out earlier to scout for any flanking–" has this moment
Sent me word that the Enemy are in the Rear of my Right
about two miles Coming Down–there is he Says about two
Brigades of them.
2 of Clock pm
He also Says he Saw a Dust Rise back in the Country
for above an hour ".[41]

By now, Howe's advance had reached Osborne's Hill,
where he halted to let his troops rest and stragglers to
catch up. "About a mile and a half directly in front, Howe
and Cornwallis could see Stephen's and Stirling's troops
moving into position, eliciting a grudging compliment
from Cornwallis, 'The damn rebels form well.' Another
British officer described the American position as 'remark-
ably strong, having a large body advanced, small bodies
still further advanced and their rear covered by a wood
wherein their main body was posted.' "[42]
Washington reacted quickly to this fresh intelligence;
and by 2:30 Sullivan had received orders to recall his
troops from the upper fords, move his division to join
those of Stephen and Stirling, and then to take command
where they met up. However, Washington's staff neglected to inform Sullivan of the exact location of Stephen
and Stirling–on the high ground around the Birmingham

---

41   Hammond, Otis G. Letters and Papers of Major–General John
Sullivan I. Concord, N.H. New Hampshire Historical Society, 1930.
p.453
42   Joseph P. Cullen. " Brandywine Creek." American History
Illustrated. August 1980. p.41

Meeting House—and Sullivan overshot them, ending up to the left of, and a half—mile closer to, the enemy than Stephen and Stirling. Sullivan caught sight of the advancing enemy just as he discovered the troops he was to join were to his rear and right. To gain time to close this gap before Howe's assault, Sullivan sent a regiment on the attack. He next hastened the rest of his men and artillery through a hollow towards the Birmingham Heights; and, then, he rode to confer with Stephen and Stirling.

Surveying the scene, the commanders agreed Sullivan should use his division to reinforce the right wing. Sullivan took overall command and transferred command of his division to his brigadier, General Prud'Homme de Borre, a French volunteer. Sullivan rode back to his division to give DeBorre the order to shift the division to the right of Stephen and Stirling, then returned to his appropriate post as overall commander of the defensive force—at the center, near the guns and overlooking both the left and right of the line. Here, Sullivan ordered the artillery to begin a sharp bombardment to cover DeBorre as he made the move to the right.

About 4PM, as their bands played "Grenadiers March", Howe's well disciplined army sallied forth from Osborne's Hill to begin their attack. For two hours—although fewer in numbers, and with less training and equipment—the Americans prevented Howe from advancing. Fighting was furious and "muzzle to muzzle". Several times the rebels were forced to give ground, but then regained it.

Terror and confusion reigned. After almost an hour, the British were near enough to launch a bayonet attack against DeBorre's element, now on the right. As they did, DeBorre panicked and fled, followed by his men. (Because of this, he subsequently resigned, rather than face a court of inquiry.)

Through it all, Sullivan valiantly directed the defense, at one point having his horse, "the best in America", shot from under him. Stirling's aide later recounted Sullivan's prowess that day:

"As I was present during the whole action...and near General Sullivan I had an opportunity of observing such examples of courage as could not escape the attention of any one. I can declare that his uniform bravery, coolness, and intrepidity, both in the heat of battle, and in rallying and forming the troops when broke from their ranks, appeared to me to be truly consistent with or rather exceed, any idea I had ever had of the greatest soldier."[43]

Eventually, the odds proved too much; and with ammunition running low—and only a few soldiers provided with bayonets–Sullivan's line began to retreat. Fortunately for the Americans, just then Nathanael Greene arrived with the reserves, General George Weedon and his brigade in the lead. As Sullivan joined Weedon's brigade, they first parted ranks to let the retreating troops pass, then reformed and began a delaying action. With volley after volley, they halted the pursuing British.

Meanwhile, the small force at Chad's Ford, under Generals Wayne and Maxwell, also put up a heroic resistance; but then, hopelessly outnumbered, they too had to withdraw.

However, "Weedon's troops were successfully buying time for the rest of the army to escape. Their fighting withdrawal slowed the British pursuit, and darkness brought

---

43   Amory, Thomas C. The Military Services and Public Life of Major–General John Sullivan. Boston, Mass.: Wiggin and Lunt,1868. p. 56

it to a standstill. Howe did send cavalry to try to cut the road to Chester, but the British troopers were beaten off by American light horse led by Polish volunteer Count Casimir Pulaski. By midnight, considerable numbers of Americans had reached the comparative safety of Chester, and the rest trickled in through the remainder of the night.

While Howe had defeated the American army, the unexpectedly bitter resistance he met had kept him from his goal of crushing it. Nor had American morale been crushed. As Washington's report to Congress stated, 'Not withstanding the misfortune of the day, I am happy to find the troops in good spirits'. " [44]

Although Congress voted the troops thirty hogsheads of rum "in compliment...for their gallant behaviour (sic)", being politicians they had to find a scapegoat for Washington only gaining a tie—even though a consequential one—and not a victory. Not surprisingly, Sullivan was once again their target.

Thomas Burke of North Carolina, one of Sullivan's inveterate enemies in the Continental Congress, made fallacious representations charging him of poor reconnaissance, misusing intelligence, and mishandling troops; and, then, he called for Sullivan to be suspended from command. To this, Washington returned a curt, sharp remonstrance; and, after learning the facts, only two in congress subsequently voted to go ahead with the suspension.

Sullivan was becoming understandably nettled at having to continuously respond to false and malicious libel and slander. Even though eventually cleared, his reaction at that time was not surprising for one, at times, consid-

---

44   John B. B. Trussel, Jr. The Battle of Brandywine". Historic Pennsylvania Leaflet. No.37. p.4

ered to be a "somewhat litigious" lawyer :

"*To his Excellency General Washington Commander in Chief of the American Army–...we*"–Generals Maxwell and Wayne were co–signers–" have severally been accus'd of unsoldierly Conduct, dangerous Neglect, and other Crimes, which, had they been prov'd, must have blacken'd our Character as Officers, and sunk us beneath the Reproaches of our Country. In Consequence of these malicious Accusations, Courts were appointed to examine into our Conduct. We patiently waited the respective Tryals, and each of us was honourably acquitted of the Charges brought against us. Since which, we have observ'd our malignant Accusers remaining in Office, without Reprimand, or Censure, triumphing at the trouble they have unjustly occasioned us, with impunity to themselves... a Court sworn to regulate their Sentence by the Articles of War must condemn every Breach of them, or give the World Liberty to accuse them of Perjury...We are by no means against General Officers being made answerable in a proper way, but we insist that when the Accusers not only fail, but appear to have made false and malicious Attack, some Punishment should be pointed out against them (sic)..[45] ....But, all this bickering would come to a head later. In the meantime, Sullivan would once again fight on the battlefield.

---

45   Hammond op. cit. pp. 580–583

CHAPTER Ten

Germantown, then Valley Forge

After Brandywine, there followed a period of maneuvering by means of which Howe was able to slip by Washington's attempts to block him— resulting in General Charles Cornwallis, with a detachment of 3500 men, occupying Philadelphia unopposed, on 26September1777. Howe remained with the bulk of the army (9500 men) which he positioned at Germantown, 5 miles above Philadelphia, to cover any likely approach of Washington's army, now encamped 30 miles northwest of Philadelphia.

At this point, the Americans were still eager for a fight. When Washington learned that the portion of the British force at Germantown had been further reduced by Howe's sending a detachment to the New Jersey side of the Delaware, he decided conditions were right to spring another surprise attack—and perhaps duplicate his success at Trenton.

His plan was clever and ambitious, although his British foes might have said too much so by half. It called for a long, complicated, night–time march south that would end with four converging prongs, divided into two wings, attacking simultaneously at 5AM, the morning of 4October1777. Sullivan was again to command the right wing. However, this time, perhaps to ward off even more controversy for Sullivan–Congress was now hashing over his performances at Staten Island and Brandywine–Washington would ride with Sullivan, rather than with Greene on the left.

Although there were two peripheral flanking attacks, at the far left and right, the key elements were to be those with Sullivan, coming down the Skippack/Germantown Road, and with Greene, attacking down the Limekiln Road.

Sullivan was at the jump–off spot at H–hour; and although Washington had not received word from Greene that he was also in place, he had Sullivan launch his attack at the designated time. Just as the sun rose–though it was to be quickly obscured by fog and smoke–his leading brigade, under General Thomas Conway, struck at the picket at Mount Airy. The British picket fell back along the Germantown Road to the cover of a solid stone mansion– "Chew House"–where they were joined by reinforcements who had hurried up to join them.

Once inside the Chew House, the British barricaded the downstairs doors and windows and manned the upstairs, turning the thick–walled building in to a veritable fortress. Sullivan therefore decided to by–pass it; and he and his lead elements, with himself in the center, Conway on the west, and Wayne on the east, continued to advance towards their objective, Market Square, in the center of Germantown, pushing the enemy before them.

However, when Washington and his staff arrived at Chew House, artilleryman Henry Knox convinced Washington that it could not be left as such in the rear of the advance. Sullivan's reserve, under General Maxwell, was ordered to take it, rather than move forward to be ready to assist Sullivan. Unfortunately, those on the staff that favored continuing Sullivan's isolate and bypass strategy should have won the argument. Knox's three pound cannon balls failed to penetrate the thick walls, and the attacking infantrymen were mowed down from inside them. This resulted not only in heavy and un–necessary American casualties; but, also, in Sullivan's not having the reserve to assist him that he had hoped for.

As the attempt to take Chew House was failing, the line of Sullivan's, Conway's, and Wayne's men was sweeping resistance before it. Howe, seeing his defense begin to disintegrate, was considering ordering the whole army to retreat to Chester, where he could be supported by the guns of the British fleet anchored there in the Delaware River. But, then, all the American mistakes of the day hit at once.

Greene's wing had become lost on the march down, which resulted in their not beginning their phase of the operation on time. This meant that as Sullivan neared their common objective, Market Square, he was un–supported on the left. Nonetheless, Sullivan penetrated to the center of town; but there resistance stiffened. Without reinforcement–his reserve was being squandered at Chew House–his attack began to falter.

Just then, Greene's portion of the attacking force belatedly came upon the scene. However, it might have been better for Sullivan if they hadn't. Instead of following his assigned line of advance along Lime Kiln Road towards Market Square, General Stephen–later cashiered for being drunk at this time–veered to the right with his brigade. Thus, instead of coming up to make contact with, and support, Wayne's left flank, his troops ended up behind it. Even worse, when, through the fog and smoke, Stephen's men dimly saw a deployed force in front of them, they opened fire, thinking those ahead were redcoats. In turn, Wayne's Continentals fired back, believing they were being attacked from the rear. Wayne, because of this–and because he thought the firing behind him at Chew House meant Sullivan had been defeated–understandably feared he was about to be cut off, and began to draw back his force. Now, Conway's left flank was exposed; and, pressed by the enemy, it also began to retreat–soon followed by Sullivan's division.

Upon hearing Sullivan's column was retreating, Greene ordered a fighting withdrawal for his. As Sullivan and Greene moved back, the other components to the attack also began to withdraw or–in just one case–were forced to surrender. There was no panic, and the retreat was made in good order. Although the British pursued for nine miles, rear guard actions by Wayne's artillerymen and Count Pulaski's cavalry allowed the Americans to get away safely.

While defeated in the end, those Americans that fought at Germantown marched away heartened and hardened, believing that, but for some unlucky breaks, their efforts would have gained a great victory. Years later, Sir George Trevelyan, writing his classic "History of the American Revolution", understood why these Americans felt they had done a great and enduring service to their cause:

"That the battle had been fought unsuccessfully was of small importance when weighed against the fact that it had been fought at all. Eminent generals, and states-men of sagacity, in every European Court were profoundly impressed by learning that a new army, raised within the year, and undaunted by a series of recent disasters, had assailed a victorious enemy in his own quarters, and had only been repulsed after a sharp and dubious conflict."[46]

Most historians believe the near success at Germantown had as much to do with France's decision to ally itself with America as did the surrender of the British army un-der Burgoyne, to Horatio Gates at Saratoga, barely two weeks later, on 17October1777. In any case, these two events certainly contributed to the surprisingly high morale of the battered army that Washington then led in to winter quarters at Valley Forge, upriver from Germantown on the banks of the Schuylkill; although there the Continentals and Washington would learn sometimes battles like Germantown aren't always the hardest thing for an army to endure.[47] (For example, as every American history stu-dent knows, after arriving at Valley Forge Washington came to realize, during the winter of 77–78, that the Congress which had time to badger Sullivan, could not get around to supplying his Continentals with basic supplies–like food.)

Sullivan felt it would be better for the Americans to attack the British again, rather than sit around starving; but nothing came of this idea. However, he was able to escape, for a while, the boredom and dreariness of the

---

46   Trevelyan, George Otto. The American Revolution. Longmans, Green & Co.1912. p.249
47   Author's Proud Note: I am a great–grandson of Elias Van Benschoten (1751–1841) who, after having been engaged at the Battle of White Plains, re–enlisted in the winter of 1777–1778 and was in General Poor's brigade at Valley Forge. Subsequently he fought in the Battle of Monmouth.

Valley Forge camp by being put in charge of building a bridge over the Schuylkill. But when that was completed, in Feb78, Sullivan felt the time was right to apply for leave—and that he had just cause for it.

Not only had he been fighting for the rebel cause the past three years, instead of earning a living—he did have a wife, family and home back in New Hampshire—he had used some of his own money to provide assistance for that cause at times; plus, in the course of the campaigns he fought in, he had lost or had stolen from him "suits of Clothes, linen, camp equipage, a military library—and three horses." In addition, his brother Ebenezer, just recently exchanged by the British, had also suffered severe financial loss serving the cause. Sullivan argued that he should have time to recoup some of his financial setbacks.

When Washington refused his request, saying he could not be spared, Sullivan replied, if that was so, why hadn't he ever been assigned a post "where there was Even a probability of Acquiring Honor". Washington answered that, on 10March78, by giving Sullivan command of the post in Rhode Island, the independent command Sullivan had always wanted. Sullivan was delighted—and gave up talk about leave.

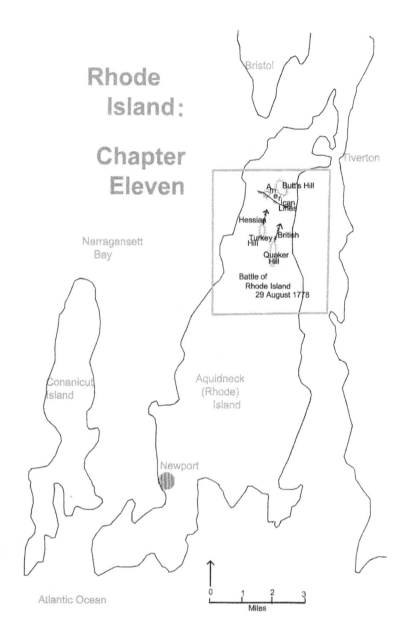

Rhode
Island:

Chapter
Eleven

Narragansett
Bay

Bristol

Tiverton

Butt's Hill

American
Lines

Hessian

Turkey
Hill

British

Quaker
Hill

Battle of
Rhode Island
29 August 1778

Conanicut
Island

Aquidneck
(Rhode)
Island

Newport

Atlantic Ocean

0   1   2   3
Miles

Eleven

Rhode Island—

An Alliance's Uneasy Beginning

Although the Continental Army under General Washington had managed to survive the Valley Forge Winter of 1777–1778, and the spring of 1778 had brought them some successes, the American situation was still quite bleak, as spring turned to summer. This was especially true in Rhode Island.

Over a year earlier, in December 1776, Aquidneck (Rhode) Island had been invaded by the English. Since then, Newport, Rhode Island's capital and her most prosperous town, had been suffering under a brutal occupation by the British and their Hessian mercenaries. In addition, British depredations blighted the state's commerce, destroyed her farms, and so impoverished the state that, by 1778, it was on the verge of famine. Acknowledging the colony's plight, Washington decided to go on the attack there that summer, to drive the British out.

As planning began, the campaign to liberate Newport,

and to open Narragansett Bay to shipping, took on an added significance. It was to be the first time American and French forces fought together as allies. In February 1778, France and the United States had signed an alliance; and, a large French fleet, with a contingent of French troops, had just arrived to assist the Americans. General Washington understood fully the importance of having a smooth beginning to this alliance, writing as he did:

"First impressions, you know, are generally longest remembered, and will serve to fix in a great degree our national character among the French."[48]

Thus, one would have thought he would have picked as the American commander for this first joint operation a general known for his tact, graciousness, and even humility—a General Eisenhower of his day. Instead, he chose a man admitted to be temperamental, overly sensitive, and hot–tempered, even by his contemporary friends and subsequent admirers.

General John Sullivan of New Hampshire, "Irish, but with neither the proverbial charm nor the luck", was to be the first American general to deal with the French in combat; and, if his friends called him "overly sensitive", others called him "contentious", "arrogant", and "vain"— some might say a Patton of his day. In addition, he had already had formal charges brought against him for his conduct at both the attack on Staten Island and the Battle of the Brandywine. However, Sullivan was not only exonerated in both cases, but commended by Washington and the Continental Congress. Indeed, in defense of General Sullivan, it should be noted that the charges—as well as

48   Hammond. Letters and Papers of Major–General John Sullivan 2. p.290

most of the invective about him—all emanated from just two bitter enemies; and, as his supporters point out:

"It should be sufficient for General Sullivan's reputation that through all the war and the following period of civil adjustment he held Washington's firm, constant, and sincere trust and personal friendship…"[49]

But, although Washington was great enough "to overlook his faults of temperament and to see and appreciate the worth of the officer and the man", even he would have agreed that Sullivan was no diplomat. Making matters worse, neither were the Frenchmen Sullivan would work with.

While the Marquis de Lafayette has now become deified in American history, at the time he was named to be one of Sullivan's two division commanders, at Rhode Island, he was a 19 year old red—head who "hope(d) a pretty decent crop of laurels may be collected upon that island". His burning desire was to be the first to lead a combined French and American force in to battle, to assuage his own personal ambition, as well as to show the Continentals "that kind of soldier that is found only among those who have French blood in their veins".[50]

Charles Hector Theodat, Count d'Estaing, the commander of all French forces, was as little thought of by his subordinates as he came to be by the Americans. "Really profound in nothing but only superficial in everything"' sniffed one of his admirals. Of course their ultimate insult, "he did not have the talents of a common sailor", reveals

49   Hammond. Letters and Papers of Major—General John Sullivan 1. p.IV
50   Gottschalk, Louis. Lafayette in America. Chicago, Ill: Univ. of Chicago, 1975. pp.242–243

that part of their ill will towards him was simply a matter of naval men resenting a former land officer turned admiral being their superior. In any case, d' Estaing and his admirals appeared at times to be the "overly sensitive" ones; and, at one crucial point in the up–coming campaign, an American lamented, they "talked like women disputing precedence in a country dance, instead of men engaged in pursuing the common interest of two great nations".[51]

Given this line–up, then, it was not surprising that bickering–over where and when the different contingents would attack–began immediately in the planning stage.

Lafayette pouted because he feared the French would play "a humiliating secondary part" and were "among people whose alien hearts would not appreciate their value".[52] He also continued to urge d' Estaing to promote his plan for a combined French and American unit, adding, "If you do me the additional kindness of asking me to command them...I will see my brightest wish fulfilled." On the other hand, the Americans, displeased with Lafayette's cajolery, felt "his private views withdrew his attention wholly from the general interest". [53]

Eventually, a compromise plan, for a simultaneous attack, by the Americans on the northeast shore of Aquidneck Island and the French on the opposite shore, was hammered out; and, while it called for Lafayette to be the first to lead a combined force, fate would intervene to prevent the realization of his dream.

---

51   Ibid pp.253 & 249
52   Ibid pp. 246 & 247
53   Ibid pp. 247 &246

〳〳〳〳〳〳

(Another Revolution first—and only—occurred in the up-coming "Battle of Rhode Island": the participation of a unit comprised of black slaves who had enlisted to fight, con-tingent upon their being freed once having passed muster. This was the First Rhode Island—"Black"—Regiment, Rhode Island's solution for having difficulty meeting its quota of troops for the Continental Army.)

〳〳〳〳〳〳

As if the relationship between the allied leaders wasn't bad enough to start with, there next occurred a chain of events that managed to make it even worse.

Because of a delay in the arrival of some of Sullivan's militia, the planned invasion date was moved back a day. D' Estaing used the extra day to review and exercise his troops on adjacent Conanicut Island. This activity alarmed the British; and, in response, they abandoned their for-tified positions in the northern part of Aquidneck Island, and concentrated their troops closer to Newport. When word of the evacuation came to Sullivan, from observers and scouts, he immediately rushed his men on to the is-land to take possession of the enemy works, before the British could decide to return to them. Having been able to take without opposition what would have cost the al-lies many casualties to take by force, Sullivan urged the French to also take advantage of the opportunity, and land right away. The French, their pride hurt by Sullivan's going first, sulked instead, causing a delay that was to ultimately prove fatal to the allied plan.

At this point, a British fleet, under Lord Howe, hove into

sight. Lord Howe, after reconnoitering the French fleet and communicating with General Pigot ashore, concluded he could not succor the town; so, the British fleet veered off and anchored in the open roadstead, leaving the French fleet and troops in the bay free to act. However, rather than persisting in the plan of attack, and putting his troops ashore, d' Estaing put to sea in pursuit of the British fleet, which cut their cables and fled on his approach.

Sullivan, left with only his "indigested body of militia and regulars"[54], decided to cautiously approach Newport and lay siege—but not assault the fortification until the French returned. After drying out from a severe two–day storm that struck 11–12August1778, the Americans advanced their lines toward Newport, constructed redoubts, and began constant and well–directed artillery fire on the British encampments.

With the siege being successfully pressed, the Americans were ecstatic to see d' Estaing and his fleet return, on 20August, feeling that now victory was assured. D' Estaing, however, immediately crushed their hopes by communicating to Sullivan his intention to leave immediately for Boston, to have his fleet, damaged during the two day storm, refitted. Sullivan, now reduced to despair, begged d' Estaing to at least cooperate with them for one or two days; but, on the 22nd, d' Estaing, admittedly under pressure from his admirals, set sail for Boston.

"Temperamental" and "overly sensitive" or not, it is easy to understand why, for Sullivan, as he later admitted to Washington, "the first struggles of passion, on so impor-

---

54   Walker, Anthony. So Few the Brave. Newport, Rhode Island. Seafield Press, 1981. p. 55

tant a disappointment, were scarcely to be restrained"[55]. Actually, they weren't restrained; and Sullivan reacted first by sending a courier in pursuit of d' Estaing, with a strongly worded and tactless letter. Although it began with an orderly argument as to why d' Estaing should at least leave his un–injured vessels and land forces, Sullivan ended by bluntly informing d' Estaing that:

"his abandoning the harbor of Newport at this time [was] derogatory to the honor of France, contrary to the intentions of His Most Christian Majesty and the interest of his nation, and destructive in the highest degree to the welfare of the United States of America, and highly injurious to the alliance formed between the two nations".[56]

This, of course, infuriated Lafayette and d' Estaing; but, Sullivan didn't stop there.

Under the spell of righteous Hibernian indignation, Sullivan further vented his feelings in the most un–diplomatic manner of all–by going public with them. In his General Orders for 24August he declared:

"Americans will prove by the event able to procure that by their own arms which their allies refuse them assistance in obtaining".[57]

Besides further angering the French–rumor at the time had it that Lafayette challenged Sullivan to a duel– this implication that d' Estaing was abandoning his allies inflamed the Americans. D' Estaing's "desertion" quickly became the talk of the camp–and then of all America. Not

---

55   Amory, Thomas C. The Military Services and Public Life of Major–General John Sullivan. Boston, Mass: Wiggin and Lunt, 1868. p.79_
56   Hammond. Op. cit. p.243
57   "Officer in the Late Army". A Complete History of the Marquis De Lafayette in the Army of the U.S.A.. Hartford, Conn.: S. Andrus and Son, 1848. p.69

only did a violent affray between some Americans and the French in Boston result in the death of one Chevalier de Saint Sauveur; but, also, in Charleston, South Carolina, an encounter between Americans and Frenchmen terminated in a formal battle, with many lives lost on both sides. "I am more upon a warlike footing in the American lines", Lafayette wrote Washington, "then when I came near the British lines at Newport". Even worse, he complained to a friend, "I have been exposed to hearing almost in my presence the name of France pronounced without respect, perhaps with contempt, by a herd of New England Yankees".[58]

Meanwhile, the "Father of our Country" had to feel like the harried father of squabbling children, as all the principals in the dispute saw fit to write and tell him their side of the story. Even today, one can just picture Washington, eagerly opening a letter from Sullivan, hoping to be told of a great allied victory, only to read:

"My Dear General—The fates have decreed that you shall receive nothing but disagreeable intelligence from this quarter".[59]

Even today, one can sense Washington's exasperation as he writes:

"I have not now time to take notice of the several arguments which were made use of, for and against the Count's quitting the harbor of Newport and sailing for Boston".[60]

Fortunately for Washington, though, if he did have a Patton on his staff, he also had a Bradley. General Nathanael Greene of Rhode Island had been named

---

58   Gottschalk op. cit. pp.259 & 261
59   Hammond op. cit. p.264
60   Officer. Op. Cit. p.70

Sullivan's second division commander (Lafayette was the other), partly because Washington felt his equanimity would balance Sullivan's tempestuousness. Greene now vindicated that decision, by assuming the role of peacemaker, even before Washington wrote to tell him:

"I depend much on your temper and influence to conciliate that animosity which, I plainly perceive by a letter from the Marquis, subsists between the American and French officers in our service...I fear it will sow the seeds of dissension and distrust between us and our new allies, unless the most prudent measures be taken to suppress the feuds and jealousies that have already arisen".[61]

By now, Lafayette felt most of his adopted compatriots were " for the most part unjust, ungrateful, selfish, lacking not only in regard to politeness, but in all impulses of the most common decency"[62]. However, he considered General Greene to be an exception; and Greene, while a friend of Sullivan, was not as displeased with Lafayette as the other American generals, for he believed Sullivan's language to have been imprudent. Greene adopted a sympathetic attitude toward the French; and he used his personal influence with Lafayette to dispel the animosity between him and the American officers—who, in turn, were convinced to put aside their passions for the good of the country. Sullivan retracted his charge that the French had refused to assist his army, and tempers subsided.

Meanwhile, forced to go on the defensive when the French left, Sullivan and the Americans successfully repulsed a major British attack in the "Battle of Rhode Island", 29August1778.

---

61   Ibid. p.71
62   Gottschalk op. cit. p.261

〄〄〄〄〄〄〄

(For the battle, Rhode Island's "Black Regiment" was amongst the elite Continentals Sullivan placed in the first line of defense. As part of the force responsible for stopping the enemy along the West Road, they were assigned to the right of the first line. There, attacking Hessians "experienced a more obstinate resistance than [we] had expected"; and, after the battle, the "Black Regiment's" white officers felt "that regiment entitled to a proper share of the honor of the day".[63])

〄〄〄〄〄〄〄

Ironically, the fleet's departure resulted in Lafayette's missing the battle—he was in Boston conferring with d' Estaing when it occurred. Despite this personal disappointment, Lafayette now showed his amiable side by calling it, "the best fought action of the war"[64].

Sullivan returned the favor, when the return of Howe's fleet necessitated a timely American withdrawal to the mainland. Lafayette arrived back from Boston August 30th; and Sullivan—sensing Lafayette was "mortify'd(sic)" to be out of action—put him in charge of the retreat. During the day of the 30th, the Americans pitched tents and worked as if fortifying their camp for a long stay; but, over the night of 30–31 August, unbeknownst to the British, all the Americans were safely ferried off the north end of Aquidneck Island to Tiverton and Bristol—once again by

---

63   Stephens, Karl F. "Color Guard". Sunday Journal Magazine. February 24, 1991. p.17
64   Simister, Florence P. The Fire's Center. Providence, Rhode Island: Rhode Island Bicentennial Foundation, 1970. p. 147

Glover's "amphibious Marbleheaders". Sullivan then wrote Congress to praise Lafayette, noting, "he did [his assignment] in excellent order, not a man was left behind, nor the smallest article lost"[65] .

So, in the end, men like Sullivan and Lafayette put aside the personal foibles they shared in order to ensure the goal they shared—a successful alliance that would lead to an English defeat. Perhaps the fact they were <u>not</u> men without fault makes their accomplishment even more noteworthy...

But, sure enough, just as this imbroglio was subsiding, Sullivan became embroiled in a quarrel of a different nature that arose during his posting in Rhode Island. All that coming fall and winter he was to complain about the inability of Congress and the Commissary Department to provide adequate forage and food for his army; and, infuriated by this, he took matters into his own hands—and had his own purchasing agents buy his supplies. In turn, irate about being by–passed, the Commissary Department decided to prosecute—as a proxy/scapegoat for Sullivan—a Captain Amasa Sessions, claiming that, while purchasing supplies in Connecticut, he had violated a Connecticut embargo when he tried to take them back to Rhode Island.

On 11March1779, Sessions was tried in Pomfret, Connecticut. Sullivan stood by his subordinate—Nathanael Greene was to later comment Sullivan might have been better occupied, but it is hard to think of "a soldier's general" doing otherwise—and acted as Sessions's lawyer. Sullivan evidently showed there was no cause for the action, as Sessions was acquitted. Then, probably because Sullivan had cause for his actions—and Washington had

---

65   Hammond op. cit. p.286

urgent need for him—the affair faded away.

Washington was asking Sullivan to lead an expedition against the Indians of the Six Nations. Once again putting duty to the cause foremost, Sullivan, despite ill health and financial worries, agreed to accept the assignment.

On Monday, 28March1779, as praise came in from fellow officers, the town of Providence, and his brother Freemasons, Sullivan—with a 13 cannon salute and accompanied by a band and many thankful citizens—left Providence for his new post.

Author's Reflections

I have devoted a significant part of this book to the forthcoming chapter on the Iroquois Campaign. Over and above the fact the expedition itself has never received the attention it deserves, it is a fitting way to show in detail much about Sullivan as a man and a leader. In the wilds of New York he will be completely out of touch with the rest of the Continental Army—every decision he makes and policy he enacts is done entirely on his own. (This, by now, admittedly favorably biased observer feels Sullivan rose to the occasion in exemplary fashion. Hopefully, the reader will agree!)

Chapter Twelve:
The Iroquois Campaign

Lakes:
Co: Conesus
H: Honeoye
Ca: Canandaigua
S : Seneca
Cy: Cayuga
Ot: Otsego

Indian Villages:
K : Kanadasaga (Geneva)
C :Canandaigua
G : Genesee Castle (Geneseo)

Routes:
S⟶ Sullivan
C⟶ Clinton
U⟶ United:
Sullivan & Clinton

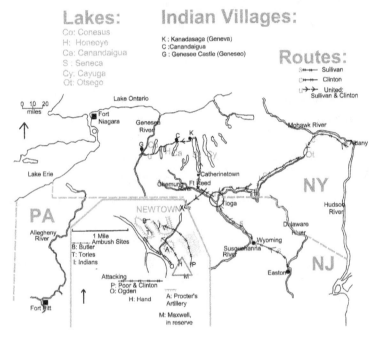

Twelve

The Iroquois Campaign

Preliminary—

It's hard today to think of George Washington, whose stately visage looked down on us benevolently from classroom walls, issuing these ruthless orders to Sullivan that would start the July–September 1779 campaign against the Iroquois in motion:

"The expedition you are appointed to command is directed against the hostile tribes of the Six Nations of Indians with their associates and adherents. The immediate objects are the total destruction and devastation of their settlements and the capture of as many prisoners of every age and sex as possible. It will be essential to ruin their crops now in the ground and preventing their planting more....[The Indian country] is not to be merely *overrun*, but *destroyed*."[66]

(On the other hand, those today aware of Sullivan's te-

---

66   Fischer, Joseph R. <u>A Well–Executed Failure</u>. Columbia, South Carolina: University of South Carolina Press, 1997. p.41

nacious competence, and his devotion to Washington and "the cause", will find it easy to understand why "the Father of our Country" became known to the hostile Iroquois as "Town Destroyer", once Sullivan had completed his mission.[67])

Going west to east, across the center of New York State, are the Seneca, Cayuga, Onondaga, Oneida, and Mohawk tribes, which were united into the "Great Peace of the Iroquois League" by Chiefs Deganawida and Hiawatha, one hundred and fifty years before European settlers began to arrive in North America. (When the Tuscarora were driven out of South Carolina in 1712, the League gave them lands adjoining the Onondaga and Oneida, thus the Iroquois became "the Six Nations".) Well organized and powerful, the Six Nations were a force to be reckoned with all during the Colonial Period.

All through the beginning of the 18th century, the Iroquois' desire was to remain neutral in the dynastic contests, hoping to manipulate all participants so as to further their own interests. However, they were not always able to do so. The Iroquois were drawn in to the "French and Indian" ("Seven Years") War on the British side; and, although they helped the British win, at its conclusion they felt their bargaining position in the region had been weakened. So, as the war between England and its colonies began, the Six Nations planned to remain neutral.

At the beginning of hostilities, both the English and the rebels wanted to keep all Indians out of the conflict. Many years later, during the winter of 1845–46, Chainbreaker, a Seneca chief during the Revolution, narrated his memories

---

67 Adler, Jeanne Winston. <u>Chainbreaker's War.</u> Hensonville, New York: Black Dome Press Corp., 2002. p.195

of that past time ; and they began with a Commissioner from the Continental Congress telling a gathering of Iroquois sachems:

"Brothers and friends, open a good ear. This is a family quarrel between us and Old England. You Indians are not concerned in it. We don't wish you to take up the hatchet against the King's troops. We desire you to remain at home and not join either side, but keep the hatchet buried deep. We ask you to love peace and maintain it, that the path may be kept open with all our people and yours, to pass and re–pass without molestation. Brothers, we live on the same ground with you; the same island is our birthplace. We desire to sit down under the same tree of peace with you."[68]

However, it wasn't long before the British began to change <u>their</u> Indian policy—especially after America's strong performance at Brandywine and Germantown, and success at Saratoga, made it clear the Continental army was not going to be quickly shattered. Then, France's entry in to the war created an even wider threat to England, causing its leaders to have to direct some of their attention to its possessions in the West Indies. All of this prompted Whitehall to change its North American strategy. They would fix the Continental army in place in the north, while detached elements of the British Army, aided by southern Loyalists, conquered the southern states. Not only would this crush the rebellion, the British hoped, it would concentrate their military forces closer to the West Indies, for the time being threatened by the French navy. For the Iroquois, this new plan meant they would now be called upon to play a significant role. Indian raids against the back coun-

---

68   Ibid pp. 38–39

try of New York and Pennsylvania would not only cause American troops to be diverted from other theaters of operation, they would disrupt an important source of food and fodder for the Continental Army.

As Chainbreaker reminisced, that winter of 1845–46, he recalled that, in addition to meetings with Americans, British Commissioners would also come to speak with the leaders of the Six Nations; but, they would urge the Iroquois to unite with them against the colonists, and to "take up the hatchet and sharp edges and paint against the enemy".[69] Moreover, before the British Commissioners would make their appeal, "officers came to us, to see what was wanted and to supply us with provisions and with the flood of rum. Some amongst our warriors made use of this intoxicating drink. The white man told us to drink as much as we wanted of it—'all free gratis'—and the goods, if any of us wished to get them for our own use, to go and get them, for 'our father has given them to you'."[70] Finally, at a council meeting in July 1777, pro–British Mohawk War Chief Joseph Brant convinced the majority of the Iroquois present—presumably after they had drunk "a flood of rum and sugar"—to go on the warpath. (Most of those assembled were from the Seneca tribe, which alone provided half of the League's warriors. They, along with the Mohawks and Cayugas, would fight as allies of the British. Although the Onondaga remained neutral, eventually the Oneida and Tuscarora agreed to aid the Americans. Consequently, the Revolution became a war that not only had white brother fighting white brother, but had red brother fighting red brother.)

---

69   Ibid p.57
70   Ibid p.51

Indian/Tory raids against the frontier settlements of New York and Pennsylvania began in the spring of 1778, continued through the summer—and in to the fall, with raids on German Flats (near Utica) in September, and Cherry Valley (near Albany) in November. But, "the mother of all raids" , the one that most shocked and terrified the frontier settlers–and caused them to flee from their farms in panic–was that in July1778, on the Wyoming Valley (near Wilkes–Barre, PA).

During June of 1778, Loyalist Colonel John Butler led a force comprised of 400 Tories and British, along with 700 to 800 Iroquois, from Fort Niagara to the area between the forks of the Susquehanna, in Pennsylvania. There, in the Wyoming Valley, the Americans had constructed a small chain of forts for protection; but, since most of the able–bodied fighters were off with the Continental Army, remaining in the Valley to man them were only 400–600 raw militia recruits, chiefly old men and boys. Ironically, though, Colonel Zebulon Butler, a Continental Army officer, was home on leave; and he took command of the Patriot force.

After securing the peaceful surrender of two small outlying forts, on 3July1778, John Butler's attacking force descended upon the major fortification in the area, Forty Fort, where Zebulon Butler and 400 militia had mustered. John Butler demanded that the Americans surrender, but Zebulon Butler refused his terms. Hearing this, John had his band pretend to withdraw, hoping to draw the militiamen out in battle. Although the experienced Zebulon urged caution, advising they wait for anticipated reinforcements before taking action, the head of the militia led his men out to pursue the enemy—and, within a couple of miles from the fort, stumbled into an ambush.

While gory details may have been added, in the re-
telling, as to what happened next, the cold facts are: the
militia broke and ran, with the Indians giving chase and
killing nearly every soldier; the Indians then burnt homes,
destroyed crops, and killed cattle throughout the Wyoming
Valley; and, finally, John Butler's force returned to Fort
Niagara with 227 scalps and only five prisoners. Even
without the stories of atrocities and fratricide that accompanied the news of the disaster, as it spread beyond the
Wyoming Valley, it is easy to understand why the Continental
Congress, and the governments of Pennsylvania and New
York, began to demand of Washington that he do some-
thing to protect America's western settlements—as if he
didn't have enough else to do.

Although under this considerable political pressure to
undertake a campaign to stop the Indian raids, Washington
was at first reluctant to do so—perhaps knowing how little cooperation he might expect from those calling for it.
But, then, he realized doing so would work in well with his
planned strategy for 1779: France's entry into the war had
created a deadlock, with the British reluctant to go on the
offensive, so Washington decided he should exhaust the
enemy by finding ways to make their stance costly –and
eventually un–sustainable. He would continue holding operations around New York to keep the British in place, while
sending a quick strike to ravage the Iroquois homelands in
central and western New York. Not only would this stop the
raids that interfered with the American supply chain; but,
since the farms and orchards of the Iroquois were produc-
ing both their own food as well as the bulk of the British
food supply, laying waste to them would not only deprive

the British of provisions, it would also make the Iroquois dependent on them, further draining their resources.

By the time he called upon Sullivan to lead this operation against the Iroquois heartland, Washington had already formulated a plan that was well–conceived, but simple—on paper, anyway. It was to be a three–pronged invasion: 1. Sullivan would lead the main body—about 3,000 men—from Easton, PA across the Pocono Plateau to Wyoming, and then from there up the Susquehanna to Tioga (Athens, PA), where the Chemung River meets the east (or north) branch of the Susquehanna; 2. Simultaneously, General James Clinton[71] , with about 1600 New Yorkers, would proceed from Albany westward to Otsego Lake, and then down the east (or north) branch of the Susquehanna to link up with Sullivan at Tioga.

From Tioga, the combined force—which, besides the infantry, would come to include artillerymen, Oneida Indian scouts, a military band, ministers, and even an unknown number of women (mostly wives of soldiers, but also some "women of the army", serving as nurses or water–carriers for the gun crews)—would ravage their way through Indian country to the Genesee Valley in western New York. There, they hoped to be joined by: 3. Colonel Daniel Brodhead, with 650 men, who would be moving north from Fort Pitt,

---

71   General James Clinton was the brother of George Clinton, the Governor of New York at that time. A son of James's, Dewitt, would be New York's Governor 1817–22—during which time he was largely responsible for the building of the Erie Canal, which traversed lands his father had helped open up for expansion. (Adding to the confusion, General Henry Clinton was then the British Commander–in–Chief in North America, having replaced Howe in May 1778. His father had been the Royal Governor of New York 1741–53, and as a boy Henry had lived in New York.)

in western Pennsylvania, along the Allegheny River to the Genesee River. (In the end, Brodhead did not keep the rendezvous, making it only to the New York State line, before having to turn back; Sullivan, of course, did not know this at the time it happened.)

In his book, "A Well–Executed Failure", Joseph R. Fischer, a U.S. Army officer and military historian, analyzes the Sullivan Campaign in terms of how well strategy, tactics, logistics, and leadership were handled. Fischer, a professor at the U.S. Military Academy from 1987 to 1990, "gives good grades" to Washington in strategy for his meticulous planning, based on the good use of available intelligence. (It is in the area of intelligence, though, that Washington could sometimes be marked down. For example, his failure to have someone reconnoiter the route between Easton and the Wyoming Valley would end up costing Sullivan time. The existing path proved inadequate for an army and its wagons to move over, and Sullivan had to have his men build a new road.)

Washington had been with Braddock when Braddock's Expedition in the French and Indian War, which was similar to what Sullivan was about to embark on, met with disaster. Because of this experience, after giving Sullivan his orders, Washington also gave him some guidance about precautions he should take, while on the march, to ensure the campaign's success; and Sullivan assiduously followed that advice. Before even starting out, Sullivan had his soldiers drilled in security measures that would deprive the enemy of the tactical advantage of surprise: how they would move and what actions they would take upon coming in contact with the enemy; crossing rivers; and, especially, avoiding ambush while passing through constricted terrain. Throughout the expedition, Sullivan employed aggressive reconnaissance patrols and strict maintenance of flank security—again, all steps to avoid surprise. He adopted a challenge and password system that would prevent confusion that might lead not only to surprise, but death by friendly fire. Because he was so successful in all this, Professor Fischer gave Sullivan top grades in tactics. (More importantly, because of his careful adherence to these dictates, in the major battle this army was to fight—at Newtown–Sullivan turned what could have been his own disaster in to victory.)

Expedition Starts———————————————

Sullivan arrived at Easton, PA on 7May1779. He immediately began assembling and training his army, while planning for its departure. As he did so, he learned the path he would leave on for Wyoming was inadequate; and he was forced to divert soldiers to road building. Slightly more than one month later, Sullivan's men had cleared—and corduroyed and bridged where necessary—forty miles of new road, the war's most impressive piece of American military engineering—but the cause of an unanticipated delay.

A month late, on 18June, Sullivan gave the order for the army to move out towards Wyoming, 65 miles away. However, even with the new road, the journey to Wyoming was hardly what one now envisions as a trip through the Poconos, as Morris Bishop describes in his clear and concise American Heritage article on the expedition:

"Wagons mired down; gun carriages broke; some horses died of exhaustion. One day only five miles were gained. It was a 'horrid rough gloomey country', wrote one soldier in his journal. And another: 'the wolves mad (sic) a wounderfool noys (sic) all around us wich (sic) Seemed Verey Destressed '(Sic). One of the dismal swamps the army traversed was aptly named 'the Shades of Death '."[72]

After six days of this tortuous travel, they finally arrived at Wyoming—but not to good news. Here, Sullivan was to discover that the one component of the endeavor that would be poorly performed was logistics. (This was primarily the responsibility not of Sullivan, but of Quartermaster General Nathanael Greene—especially since Sullivan had just arrived in this theater of operations, and almost all of the regiments were new to his command.)

Although Greene had many problems of his own to deal with in doing his job, the bottom line was: most of the beef supply had spoiled, as it was packed in casks that leaked their brine, a result of being made of green wood; cattle that were supposed to accompany the march could not even stand; anticipated clothing, shoes, blankets, and tents had not arrived; there was a shortage of gunpowder; local farmers, whom Sullivan was there to help, refused to rent pasture or sell forage; and, finally, those same locals refused to lend wagons or act as wagoners.

Washington— who was somewhat un–realistically thinking in terms of a lightning strike type of raid—and Greene and his minions—for obvious reasons of their own—responded to the problem by adopting a "what's the big deal about taking off in to the wilderness without proper supplies—just play it by ear" attitude. But Sullivan, knowing full well what it was like to be blamed for the

72 Bishop, Morris. "The End of the Iroquois". American Heritage. October 1969. pp.31–32

mistakes of others, was not about to be rushed in to going forward until he was certain the soldiers he was responsible for could be properly clothed and fed.

Instead, in characteristic fashion, Sullivan set about trying to correct the problems himself. Unable to make good the clothing shortage from nearby Pennsylvania and New York, he managed to convince Washington to have clothes, shoes, and stockings shipped from depots as far away as Boston—though much of it never arrived. Attempts to salvage some of the spoiled meat were unsuccessful; all that could be done in this regard was to try and detect the defective barrels as early in the supply chain as possible, in order to save precious carrying space for meat that was eatable. Having soldiers hunt—and especially fish the teeming Susquehanna—provided a small amount of relief; but Sullivan looked to increasing his herd of cattle as the most important part of the solution, and here he did have some success. In the end, though, even Sullivan accepted the fact he would have to also forage the Six Nations to ensure that his men and animals were adequately fed—although knowing doing so would cause delays.

So it was, that, during the afternoon of 31 July 1779, Indian sentinels, in the hills above the "Warriors' Path" (present–day Highway 6), watched as "a long blue snake"[73] set out, heading north up the Susquehanna towards Tioga. Six miles long, Sullivan's column was accompanied by 700 head of cattle, 1,200 pack horses, and 120 bateaux (light and flat–bottomed boats, which carried most of the meat). Operational security was not a factor;

---

73   Eyres, Lawrence E. "Sullivan's Expedition Against the Iroquios (sic)". <u>The Chemung Historical Journal.</u> December 1959. p.653

rather, Sullivan counted on the size and boldness of his army to have a disheartening effect on his foes. Apparently it did, because the procession made it through the 80 tortuous miles unmolested, arriving at Tioga on 11 August. Although the soldiers knew they were being watched, and expected to be attacked at any time, fighting the rapids and strong current of the river, and the rough terrain of the steep mountainsides along it, proved to be the biggest battle of the march.

Actions Vicinity of Tioga

As soon as the army had begun to set up camp at Tioga, to await the arrival of Clinton's element, Sullivan sent an eight–man reconnaissance mission up the Chemung River. Heading out at dusk, it worked its way slowly north during the night. Early in the morning, the patrol came to some high ground that overlooked the Indian village of Chemung. Un–detected, they spent the morning observing. Below, between two and three hundred Tories and Iroquois were engaged in a flurry of activity; but, the scouts were unable to determine if they were preparing to evacuate the village, or go on the offensive. About mid–day, the patrol slipped away and hurried back the twelve miles to Tioga.

Late in the afternoon of August 12th, the scouts arrived back at Tioga and gave their report to Sullivan. Sullivan gathered his key subordinates for a council of war, which promptly decided the situation called for a pre–emptive strike against Chemung the next morning.

That evening, leaving two regiments behind to guard the camp, most of Sullivan's force set out to undertake the "hammer and anvil" plan he had devised. For the "anvil",

General Hand and his light infantry brigade were to pass around the village and block escape routes to the north, Colonel George Reid would take two regiments across the Chemung to prevent escape to the west, and Sullivan would position himself with three New Jersey regiments and some artillery south of the village. As the "hammer", General Poor and his brigade would attack the village from the east. It was an excellent plan, especially considering it was worked out so quickly, and it almost worked–even though it required precise timing, while operating at night in difficult and unknown terrain.

However, as often happens in war, things didn't go as planned once the operation started. Not only was it arduous going, many units became lost; and, as a consequence, instead of Poor attacking before dawn, it was after sunrise when Hand's advanced units reached the village—only to find it deserted. Then, hearing cowbells to the north, Hand's detachment took off in pursuit of the presumed fleeing enemy–a little too exuberantly. Those in front were caught in an ambush; and six were killed and nine wounded before the remainder of the pursuing party—their training kicking in— moved to flank the ambush position, causing the ambushers to withdraw.

To make sure Chemung could no longer support a force large enough to threaten the camp at Tioga, the Colonials burned its forty dwellings and the surrounding fields. Then, carrying the dead and wounded, the army returned to Tioga, arriving back by nightfall. Here, while continuing to wait for Clinton's New York Brigade, they built a four–blockhouse fort, Fort Sullivan, which would be used for the defense of those elements that were to remain at Tioga. Sullivan sited it at "the carrying place", a canoe portage from the Susquehanna to the Chemung, across the narrowest spot on the Tioga peninsula. This provided a water barrier on the Fort's west and east sides; and, to the north and south, Sullivan had the trees cleared away to provide an un–obstructed view–and a clear field of fire for the six–pound cannons that would eventually end up being left behind.

Meanwhile, although Sullivan was becoming concerned, General James Clinton and his men were safely on their way, after a very ingenious start.

Clinton, alerted by Washington the beginning of spring 1779, had begun his move in June. With 212 bateaux, built especially for the campaign, his force moved up the river to Canajoharie. From there, the bateaux were carried by wagon twenty–five miles overland to Otsego Lake, on a road prepared by Clinton, a surveyor and engineer by profession. On the 17th of June, the New Yorkers put their boats in the water at the north end of Otsego Lake and paddled them to its southern outlet, where the East Branch of the Susquehanna begins (near present–day Cooperstown). "There he encamped to await orders from General Sullivan. The delay was fortunate. The water in the upper reaches of the Susquehanna was too shallow to carry the boats. Clinton found a simple yet clever solution: he built a temporary dam at Otsego's outlet. The lake level rose slowly; in six weeks it gained two feet, while the river below dwindled almost to nothing."[74]

On August 4th, a messenger from Sullivan arrived with the order to start for the rendezvous at Tioga. On the evening of the eighth, the dam was broken; the next morning,

---

74 Bishop. Op. Cit. p.33

the bateaux, with the supplies, were launched, and started floating downstream, accompanied by Clinton's 1500 men marching overland. Ahead of them, the Indians, taking this diminution of the river, followed by a sudden flood, to be the work of "the Great Spirit"—and a bad omen—fled from their villages, which were then put to the torch by the soldiers as they passed through.

As Clinton, heading south, neared Tioga, he was met on 19August by General Poor and his brigade, which a worried Sullivan had dispatched to clear the way for Clinton. On the twenty–second, Poor led Clinton on to Tioga Point, to be welcomed by a 13 gun salute and "a Band of Musick (sic) which played Beautiful".

Four days later, on 26August1779, leaving a detachment behind under Colonel Israel Shreve to accumulate a food depot, the combined force left Fort Sullivan, headed for Indian country along the Chemung River. Ahead of them, Colonel Butler—with his green–coated Tory rangers—and Mohawk Chief Brant were preparing the Indians[75] in the area to oppose the coming invasion of their homeland. (Their combined force was about 700.) Butler and Brant favored a series of delaying actions; but the assembled chiefs—who were beginning to question just how much help they really could count on in the future from the British—favored making a major stand before the Delaware village of Newtown.

For the ambush site, the Delaware chiefs chose a spot where the trail coming north, along the Chemung, passes between a long narrow ridge on the left and a high spur on

---

75   This included not only Iroquois, but their Delaware allies, whose villages in the area would be the first to be reached by the American Army.

the right. Forming the heart of the ambush, Sixty Tory rangers, with thirty Iroquois led by Brant, were placed along the ridge, while across from them warriors occupied the lower levels of the spur. Butler, with the rest of the rangers, and the few British regulars present, held the center. Most of the remainder of the Indians were placed along the top of the spur to guard against the Colonials attempting to flank their position, as well as to be ready themselves to flank Sullivan. After fortifying their hiding places, the ambushers further concealed them with fresh cut saplings and branches. During the evening of the 27th, they settled in to await their target; and, all through the 28th, and during the morning of the 29th, wait they did. Warriors became bored and careless, in some cases moving from their assigned positions; in the August heat, the camouflaging foliage began to wither.

Late the morning of 29 August 1779, Sullivan's reconnaissance force, a detachment of "Morgan's Riflemen" led by Major James Parr, came to a location near Newtown where the woods gave way to head–high grass. Parr signaled his men to halt, and then sent one of them up a tree to get a better look ahead. From his tree–top perch, the observant scout detected a spot in the distance where faded leaves stood out in contrast to the bright green backdrop. Looking closer, he espied through a gap in the camouflage a flash of red—a war–painted Indian!

Sullivan, arriving at the scene, was given this intelligence. Quickly, he planned a classic double envelopment, hoping to achieve a decisive victory, and completely destroy his foe. General Hand would fix the enemy in position, supported by Colonel Proctor's artillery, the artillery being set up on a small knoll 400 yards in front of the ambush position. Generals Poor and Clinton, with their brigades, would circle around to the right, cross over the spur—clearing it of any enemy posted there—and then descend upon the enemy's left flank and rear. Colonel Ogden and his New Jersey regiment would move along the river and take up positions behind the enemy's right flank, ready to sally forth once the battle began. The rest of General Maxwell's brigade would be held in reserve. Artillery would add "shock and awe": Riflemen would keep up a slow fire—just enough to "amuse" the enemy— to keep them from "discovering" the artillery's placement; then, in dramatic fashion, its presence would suddenly become known to the Indians when it opened fire—which would be the signal for Poor and Clinton to attack the enemy below.

For a double envelopment to work, there has to be precise timing—and luck. (Sullivan's army would have neither this day, from a strict tactical sense; but, strategically, it would be a success.) Soon after setting off on their sweep to the right, the Clinton/Poor element was forced to spend time wading through an unexpected swamp. Per plan, a half–hour after they had jumped off, the artillery opened fire; but Poor was then only starting the climb up the spur, while Clinton was still at the bottom. Poor, knowing he was behind schedule, rushed his already exhausted men to the spur's crest. There they were met by intensive firing, which momentarily stunned the Continentals. Regaining control, Poor led a bayonet charge that quickly sent his opponents fleeing. But, now, the ambushers had been alerted to the threat coming from their left; and the Indians realized they might be cut off from escaping. Moreover, as Butler later wrote, "the [artillery] shells bursting beyond [behind] us made the Indians imagine the enemy had got their artillery around us and so startled and confused them that a greater part of them ran off...many made no halt, but proceeded immediately to their villages"[76]. Tories, as well as Indians, then fled up the Chemung before the victorious Colonials.

Sullivan lost only three dead and thirty–nine wounded, with all but four of the casualties coming from Poor's brigade. Butler had five of his men killed and three wounded. While twelve Indian dead were found on the battlefield, their total number of casualties would never be known, since they took them when retreating. "But wars are not necessarily decided by body counts. Newtown was one of the decisive battles of the Revolution. Its character and outcome so terrified the Iroquois that they would never again meet the invaders in battle [in force]. The unhappy fate of the great Iroquois Confederacy was decided at Newtown; the battle monument [on Sullivan's Hill] is the gravestone of the Iroquois civilization."[77]

Their morale soaring, Sullivan's men spent 30August "industriously employed in destroying Newtown... [including] about 150 acres of what one soldier noted was 'the best corn I ever saw' "[78] .

As for evaluating Sullivan's execution of the "Battle of Newton", who better to do it than his adversary, Colonel Butler:

"[Sullivan's soldiers] are some of the best of the Continental Troops *commanded by the most active of the rebel generals* (this author's italics) ...They move with the

76   Fischer. Op. Cit. p.92
77   Bishop. Op. Cit. p.78
78   Adamiak, Stanley J. "Sullivan's 1779 Campaign". The Chemung Historical Journal. June, 2004. p.5481

greatest caution and regularity & are more formidable than you [Lt. Col. Bolton, commander at Niagara] seem to apprehend"[79] .

Through Iroquois Territory

Before leaving Newtown, Sullivan made two key decisions: 1. Considering the difficulties incurred just in bringing the artillery from Tioga to Newtown, Sullivan was convinced "that the transport [of the artillery and supporting wagons] to the Genesee [was] impracticable and absurd as an attempt to level the Alleghany [sic] mountains"[80] . He sent back to Tioga the four six–pounders he had with him, leaving him with three small cannons, the largest a three–pounder. (Which proved to be a wise decision, as the results of Newtown obviated the call for heavy artillery during the rest of the campaign.); 2. Noting the abundance of food they were finding in the Indian towns, Sullivan asked his soldiers to accept half–rations, and to forage off enemy stores to supplement their diet. "The soldiers unanimously proclaimed their readiness with three rousing cheers. The General was touched by 'this truly noble and virtuous resolution.' "[81] (Of course, Sullivan's promise to reimburse them in pay for the missed meals may have had much to do with the soldiers acquiescing so enthusiastically!)

On August 31st, after destroying more corn at the Indian village of Kanawahalla (Elmira), the column left the Chemung and headed north on a night march towards Catherine's Town, hoping to catch by surprise some Iroquois

---

79   Fischer. Op. Cit. p.101
80   Ibid pp.83–84
81   Bishop. Op. Cit. p.78

believed to have fled there. Struggling to make their way through a pitch–black night, they became further bogged down when they encountered an eight mile long, nearly impenetrable, hemlock swamp. At dawn, the advance party emerged from the swamp and arrived at Catherine's Town. There, they found that Queen Catherine[82] and her subjects had fled minutes before, leaving behind—besides horses, cows, calves, and hogs–only an old Indian woman. As the mud splattered troops continued to plod in to the town throughout the day, they set about burning its 30 houses, corn fields, and fruit orchards. However, Sullivan—holding to the ethical high ground when it came to the treatment of noncombatants–had the old woman provided with a bark cabin and six weeks provisions.

From here, the army advanced northward along the eastern shoreline of Seneca Lake. Although they continued to burn deserted dwellings and crops, and to girdle or chop down peach and apple trees, Sullivan was now leaving some fields of corn and vegetables untouched, knowing that at least part of his army would have to return along the same route.

As the Continentals approached Kanadesga (or Canadasaga) ,the capital of the Seneca Nation, located just northwest of present–day Geneva, they feared an ambush. Conditions there, at the outlet of Seneca Lake, were ideal for one. Just a mile from the large village, they would have to cross a twenty–yard wide, waist–deep rapid river, bordered by a marsh that could provide plenty of cover for waiting warriors. Moreover, they had been told a force of

---

82   Queen Catherine (Montour) was a half breed French/Huron who had been captured by the Iroquois. She was married to a Seneca chief, and after his death she became a leader of the tribe.

a thousand warriors was resting there.

Sullivan was prudent as always; and, his soldiers were well trained. Approaching the river crossing, he sent out scouts to "reconnoiter the ground". As they had practiced at Easton, the troops formed up covering parties while crossing the river. Once they had crossed the river, they quickly surrounded the town. But an attack never came, and the town was empty. Terrified by the advancing horde, the Indians could not be induced by Butler to make a stand. Kanadesaga, with 70 to 80 houses, was the largest town yet. While it was undergoing the routine destruction, Sullivan dispatched parties to burn some outlying villages.

Then on to Canandaigua (Kanandaiqua), at the north end of Canandaigua Lake, arriving on the 9th of September. Many houses there had signs on the doors proclaiming, "he who destroys this house his offspring shall suffer for it"[83]. Not cowed, the soldiers quickly destroyed the town's thirty "elegant" houses, and fifty acres of fields, while its women and children hid on Squaw Island.

Next, on 11September, the Continental swarm descended upon Honeoye, at the north end of that lake, surprising a small group of Indians that " 'Just made their escape', leaving behind their 'Packs & Blankets & Potatoes Roasting in the fire' ".[84]

By this time, Sullivan had decided the campaign of destruction should proceed as far as the great Genesee Castle (Geneseo), the largest Seneca town, located just west of the Genesee River. Not only would this guarantee his men enough food for the return to Tioga, Sullivan was still hoping to meet up with Brodhead's force out of

---

83   Adamiak. Op. Cit. p.5484
84   Ibid p.5484

Pittsburgh. Sullivan's plan now was to leave most of the pack horses and supplies, and one of the three–pounders, at Honeoye, under the care of a small garrison contingent; so that the main component of his force could move faster, and catch the Iroquois at Genesee Castle off–guard.

Arriving at the south end of Conesus Lake, Sullivan and the attacking force found they had to then cross a stream and a quaking bog–and that Butler had burned the bridge across the stream. Perhaps because Sullivan recalled how long it took to slog through the swamp before Catherine's Town—and also knew there was always the chance they might have to beat a hasty retreat back the same way—Sullivan felt it would be best to take the time to re–build the bridge and construct a causeway. He also decided to utilize this time sending out a small patrol, to find the exact location of Genesee Castle, and the best route to it.

On 13September1779, Sullivan assigned Lieutenant Thomas Boyd[85] to accomplish the scouting mission. Boyd was told to take no more than three or four Colonials, along with Oneida Chief Hanyost Thaosagwat (Hanyara) and a few Indians. He was instructed to observe only—not call attention to themselves by attempting to take scalps—and

---

85 Spiegelman, Robert. "In Sullivan/Clinton's Wake; Part2". Chemung Historical Journal. March 2005. p.5582 :Historian Jerod Rosman describes the ambitious Boyd as "an accident looking for a place to happen". Rosman's research further reveals that, as Boyd was preparing to leave Schoharie, New York, a Miss Cornelia Becker caught hold of him and beseeched him to marry her, declaring that if he didn't "she hoped he would be cut to pieces by the Indians". Boyd drove the woman off with his sword; and, as she left, she "call[ed] down the vengeance of heaven upon him". After Boyd's death, Miss Becker gave birth to a girl that grew up to be a respected and happily married woman.

to return to camp before daybreak the next day. (Standard procedure was to return via a different route.)

Boyd started taking liberties with Sullivan's orders immediately, taking twenty–six men, " a much larger number than I had thought of sending and by no means so likely to answer the purpose as that which had been directed"[86], Sullivan later reported to Congress. Then, finding an empty Indian village, Boyd committed his second violation of orders: sending four men back to report his discovery, Boyd and the rest hid, planning to kill any returning enemy. When four Indians on horseback rode into the village, Boyd's party opened fire, resulting in one being killed, by marksmen Timothy Murphy, but the rest escaping to sound the alarm.

Boyd then began a leisurely retreat back along the same route they had come, even further violating orders by making the decision, after only a few miles on the trail, to halt and await Sullivan's arrival, rather than return to camp before daybreak. He does send two messengers back to inform Sullivan he has countermanded his orders, but before long they return to tell Boyd there are several Indians on the trail ahead of them.

Hanyara warns Boyd of a trap; but, Boyd takes off in pursuit of the hostile Indians, who flee towards an ambush site Butler already has in place to catch Sullivan's force, once they leave the site of the burned bridge. Boyd leads his men right in to it, and nearly four hundred Indians and Tories overwhelm his patrol. Only a few men, sent around the right flank of the ambush, escape.

General Hand's soldiers, in the front of the advance, hear the sound of battle a half–mile away, and quickly

---

86   Bishop. Op. Cit. p.79

rush to drive the ambushers away. Arriving after Butler's men have departed, the relief party beholds fourteen corpses among the trees, including that of a dismembered Hanyara—and also realizes Boyd and Private Michael Parker are missing, and presumed captured.

Although Boyd's patrol was a bungled one, that was fatal for those on it, it served their fellow campaigners well, by causing Butler's ambush to be sprung before they fell into it. "Having lost the advantage of surprise, and being greatly outnumbered, Indians and Tories turned and fled westward, nor did they stop until they reached Niagara."[87]

Now with added impetus, the Americans marched at full speed towards Genesee Castle, debouching upon it during the afternoon of 14 September. There they found the mutilated corpses of Boyd and Parker. With a vengeance, their comrades–in–arms spent the next two days razing the town, which was now the largest they had seen. One Hundred and Twenty–Eight "large and elegant" houses and 20,000 bushels of corn were burned, "with great cheerfulness".

Return and Assessment

On the 16th of September, 1779, Sullivan issued an order that said:

"The Commander–in chief informs his brave and resolute army that the immediate objects of this expedition are accomplished, viz: total ruin of the Indian settlements and the destruction of their crops, which were designed for the support of those inhuman barbarians, while they

---

87   Bishop Ibid. p.79

were desolating the American frontiers. He is by no means insensible to the obligations he is under to those brave officers and soldiers whose virtue and fortitude have enabled him to complete the important design of the expedition, and he assures them he will not fail to inform America at large how much they stand indebted to them. The army will this day commence its march for Tioga."[88]

On the 17th, Sullivan's men reached Honeoye, where they gathered their supplies and the small detachment that had been left there. Burning along their way anything they had missed, the army then retraced its steps to Kanadesaga, at the top of Seneca Lake. There, on September 20, Sullivan divided his force to cover more territory.

One section, of 100 men, under Colonel Peter Gansevoort, was sent eastward to Albany, along the Mohawk Valley. Along the way, besides destroying enemy villages, they surprised the lower Mohawk Castle and took all of its inhabitants prisoner. They arrived, with the prisoners, at Albany on Oct. 2.

At the same time, and to accomplish the same purpose, Colonel William Butler led 600 men down the east side of Cayuga Lake, while Colonel Henry Dearborn took 200 down the west side. Both of the detached elements then headed for the Tioga area to re–join Sullivan's component.

Sullivan sent a contingent from his force to sweep the west side of Seneca Lake; and he covered the now desolated eastern side of Seneca Lake with the rest. In Catherine's Town, Sullivan replenished the old squaw's provisions. (While this act brought tears of gratitude to her eyes, it drew mixed emotions from the soldiers.) Farther

---

88   Eyres. Op. Cit. p.660

on, after emerging from the long swamp, some of the pack horses were in such bad condition that about one hundred were shot. (Later, for some reason, Indians arranged the skulls along the path, whence the name of present–day Horseheads, New York.)

On September 24, Sullivan marched in to Fort Reed (Elmira), which had been built as a food depot during his absence; and then, within two days, the detachments sent around Cayuga also arrived. Full rations were restored–and fun was had by all! Five gallons of spirits were distributed, and a day of celebration "closed 'with civil mirth' and with appropriate toasts, such as 'May the kingdom of Ireland merit a stripe in the American standard' and 'May the enemies of America be metamorphosed into pack horses, and sent on a western expedition against the Indians'."[89]

During the morning of September 29, the army destroyed Fort Reed, then began the march downstream to Fort Sullivan. There, on the 30th, another party was held, beginning with a repeat of a *feu de joie* , performed at Fort Reed. (This maneuver calls for each soldier to fire his musket in succession, with only a fraction of a second between shots, then return to order arms. When Sullivan galloped down the line of soldiers, with a rolling musket fire just behind him, it created such an impressive sight the assembly burst in to cheers.) Then, amongst much feasting on fat bullocks, officers wearing paint were led in an Indian dance by an Oneida sachem, screaming a war whoop at the end of each measure. (Don't you kind of wish you had been there?!?)

Fort Sullivan was destroyed on the third of October; and, the following day, the army set out downstream

89   Bishop. Op. Cit. p.80

to Wyoming—mostly by boat, another cause for bliss. Reaching Wyoming on the 7th, they then left for Easton on the 10th. On 15 October1779, the army arrived at Easton; and, even though the local tavern keepers had "stocked their establishments to the gills with liquor", expecting the in–coming soldiers to break ranks and "head for the bars", Sullivan's well–disciplined Continentals marched past the temptations and to their campgrounds. (No doubt, though, the soldiers helped the innkeepers get rid of their liquor supply after they were dismissed!)

In his book, Joseph R. Fischer deems Sullivan's campaign a "Failure", even though "Well–Executed", due to the fact that, in the Spring of 1780, the Iroquois resumed their raids in Pennsylvania and New York. Nevertheless, that seems to be like calling "The Battle of Midway" a failure for the United States because Japan continued to fight for three more years. Just as Japan's naval/naval aviation strength in the Pacific was severely and irreparably weakened, so too was the ability of the British to wage war in the Northeast, once their Iroquois allies were irreparably weakened—and became almost as much a liability as a strength.

Because Sullivan was on the offense at the time, the western communities were spared from attack during the critical growing and harvesting period of 1779. By the same token, not only were the British denied food they usually obtained from the Iroquois, the British became obliged to care for the devastated Iroquois during the harshly cold '79–'80 "Winter of Hunger". This not only brought comparative peace to the frontier that winter and early spring, it undermined the British capability to wage war that coming campaign season. And, just as one can only imagine, in horror, how much more damage the Japanese could have wrought upon the Americans if they hadn't lost 4 carriers and 248 aircraft at Midway; so, too, one can only imagine how much more suffering the Iroquois could have wreaked upon the Americans if the Six Nations had been as unified and formidable that Spring of '80, as they were before Sullivan completed his mission.

Anyway, for a final word regarding Sullivan's performance throughout it all, we can return to Fischer's critique. We have already noted that Fischer judges Sullivan to have done well tactically. He then concludes that Sullivan possessed many of the qualities that make one a great officer and a leader of men in war.

Feeling that the Continental Army championed an aggrieved and righteous people, Washington expected its officers to maintain high ethical standards, and to instill those standards into the army as a whole. During the course of the campaign, Sullivan did so, by example, on several occasions. Although it is easy to understand soldiers pilfering from the farmers of Pennsylvania as the campaign began—especially considering how little support the State of Pennsylvania was providing—Sullivan made it clear to his soldiers that, regardless of circumstances, an army of the people could not be the people's oppressor. Despite passions becoming inflamed amongst the ranks upon hearing the stories of the Wyoming Massacre, and despite the fact Sullivan had been given the order to wage total war on hostile Indians using famine as an objective, Sullivan held to the ethical high ground when otherwise dealing with Indians. His concern about the treatment of non–combatants was epitomized by his treatment of the old squaw at Catherine's Town; and Sullivan, on several occasions, instructed his officers not to tolerate soldiers verbally abusing the Oneida, Tuscarora, and Stockbridge Mohican Indians who were acting as guides.

A good officer: shows concern for his soldiers—and that he is willing to share their hardships—while, at the same time, he maintains firm but fair discipline; and he motivates his men to accomplish the task he assigns them.

Sullivan showed the army he had their welfare in mind in the way he had them go on half–rations at the end of August, making it a request, rather than an order. (True, he worded it so as to elicit approval, but it was made in good faith; anyone not concurring could return to Tioga.) He showed he was willing to do what he asked of others when, later on the march, a shortage of packhorses necessitated first his cavalry–and then his officers–to dismount. Although suffering from gout, Sullivan joined them in walking the rough terrain.

While Sullivan adhered to strict discipline—he convened courts–martial frequently–he tried to balance it with realism: for example, when it came to the theft of food, first offenders usually received light punishments, and were often pardoned. While he would "never countenance Soldiers in disrespectful behavior to officers", he could "never suffer officers to beat and abuse their soldiers wantonly". (And what better display of discipline could there have been than when, arriving at Easton, at the end of it all, the army held its ranks marching past the liquor–stocked taverns!)

A Deist[90] , for motivation Sullivan started with religion.

90 Fischer. Op. Cit. p.146. Chaplain Kirkland wrote his wife that

He actively encouraged his chaplains to remind soldiers they fought for a righteous cause blessed by God. Along with religion and discipline—"God and the lash"—Sullivan used ceremony to build esprit de corps. From reviews at Easton and Wyoming, at the beginning, to the *"feu de joie"* at the end, Sullivan used military display to convince his army, as much as anyone, of its own competence and ability.

In sum, Sullivan "led the army forward not through a reliance on fear, but, rather, on the development of a sense of unit cohesion and spirit..."[91]. Sullivan may have been a man "not without his faults"; but, not being a great leader of men in war was not one of them.

Sullivan had once been an Atheist, but was now a Deist—"of which there is no want in the Army". (Even then, "there are no atheists in the foxholes".)
91   Ibid p.155

Thirteen

Civilian Life

As the focus of the war shifted south, where it would come to its climax at Yorktown, 19October1781, Sullivan felt the time was finally right to rehabilitate his physical and financial well–being. Over the course of November, 1779, he submitted to the Continental Congress–and had accepted–his resignation; and, while it is often said Congress accepted it eagerly because they were tired of Sullivan's complaining, perhaps Sullivan was equally fed up with Congress's constant harassment of him.

In what must have felt like a most welcome change, he was greeted with adulation upon his return to his home state of New Hampshire, in December 1779. During the winter of 1780, the President (Governor) of New Hampshire and the Speaker visited him to wish him well with the mending of his health; and he was brought from his home in Durham to speak before the New Hampshire Council and Assembly, where he received an ardent reception.

"As his health improved, Sullivan got his law practice

going again, 'to repair the repeated & almost inconceivable Losses' he had sustained. By May he was advertising that his mills once more were operating and suited for dying silks and dressing cloths. Although he seemed to be making an easy transition into the activities of his community, he could not remain in Durham for long. Against his desire, the legislature chose him as a delegate to the Continental Congress, to serve one year beginning in November 1780."[92]

Sullivan had been selected while out–of–state; but, since he realized it would be expensive for the state to re–call another legislative session to replace him—and knew his state needed a firm voice in Congress to present its case in disputes with New York over land west of the Connecticut River–he reluctantly returned to the Continental Congress. Once there, seeing the need for fiscal stability–and for restoring order out of the chaos of wartime finance–he spent most of his time working on the country's economic problems… However, though toiling diligently—even while suffering from a "fever epidemic" raging in Philadelphia —controversy would again haunt him.

Despite the inauspicious start to their relationship during the Battle of Rhode Island, Sullivan liked the French, spoke their language, and had become friends with Marbois, the French charge d'affairs. Having this viewpoint, from the beginning of his stay in Congress–and unlike most of the other New Englanders—he had been in opposition to the anti–Gallician clique led by Arthur Lee and Samuel Adams; but, while he always supported the French, he also used this friendship, in turn, to press them for financial aid for America.

---

92 Whittemore Op. Cit. p.153

Learning of Sullivan's money problems, Chevalier de la Luzerne, the French minister at Philadelphia, wanting to make sure this valuable ally was able to remain in Congress, loaned Sullivan money from his own pocket, some time in late 1780 or early 1781. Around this same time, France, increasingly distressed by the cost of the war, and also feeling there might be a better chance for a compromise to end it if the intractable John Adams wasn't the only American peace commissioner abroad, was pushing for him to at least be joined by others, one from each section of the country. On 15June1781, Congress voted for Adams to become one of five commissioners. As it turned out, "with Jay [NY] in Spain, Henry Laurens [Deep South] locked up in the Tower of London, Jefferson [VA] unlikely to leave Virginia, and Adams [New England] tied down with his assignment in Holland, there remained only Franklin [PA] to serve as the American negotiator at Paris"[93]. It was exactly the result the French desired; and, while Sullivan had voted for it, so had the vast majority of Congress. Never–the–less, this fact was used in a subsequent charge that Sullivan took a bribe.

Another episode used to support this bribery charge—believe it or not!–concerns Sullivan's meeting with his older brother, Daniel–dying from incarceration aboard a British prison ship. Daniel was sent as a pawn to Philadelphia, in May 1781, to deliver an overture of peace from the British[94]. Sullivan discussed with Luzerne ways this might be used to spare his brother further imprisonment, as well as

---

93 McCullough, David. <u>John Adams.</u> New York: Simon & Schuster, 2001. p. 261
94 In: Whittemore. Op. Cit. pp. 169–173, is to be found a very detailed and interesting account of all this.

to bait a trap for the British; but, then, his brother died, and nothing came of it—except further charges that Sullivan had been on the take !!

(Note: In the late 19ᵗʰ Century, in response to this charge being made once again by the early 19ᵗʰ Century historian George Bancroft, the New Hampshire Historical Society appointed a distinguished committee to look in to these allegations. Their findings cleared Sullivan.[95])

Moreover, many members of Congress, who had only been talking while Sullivan was fighting, continued to regard as "whining" Sullivan's not un–reasonable request they "make good" on money he deserved. So, on 11 August 1781, a much miffed John Sullivan left Congress and headed back to the "friendly confines" of New Hampshire, which, as a war hero–with a knack of leadership, ability to persuade, and the courage to face crises unflinchingly–he would serve well over the next nine years.

His first task in the service of New Hampshire, beginning in September 1781, was working with others to establish an efficient state government. Here he found it was necessary to balance his belief a government should be controlled directly by the people with the reality that a strong executive branch was needed for efficiency. This argument over a plan of government, New Hampshire's Constitution, continued through 1782 and in to 1783; and, it was not until October, 1783, that it was approved.

During this time he assumed the duties of New Hampshire's Attorney General, a post he held from September 1782 until 1786. (Although he also continued

---

95 Authored by "distinguished 19ᵗʰ century NHHS members", Bell et. Al., it appears in NHHS proceedings, Volume 1 (1872–1888), pp. 95–104.

his law practice—being excused by Superior Court from acting in cases he was involved in—and to oversee his mills.)

In the summer of 1783, Sullivan's performance as AG came under attack by some who claimed he was not pressing for the sale of confiscated Loyalist estates. He countered, with much legal language, that grand juries had not found bills in this matter; and, therefore, it was not his place to act without them. Then, In December of 1783, he undertook his most difficult assignment as AG: traveling to Annapolis to argue before the Continental Congress, meeting there, New Hampshire's assertion that, in maritime cases, a Court of Appeals established by Congress should not have precedence over New Hampshire's judiciary. Sullivan presented his case so effectively the committee that considered the matter reported in his favor; but, the matter died on 30March1784, when not enough votes could be mustered to pass the committee's opinion in the form of a resolution.

However, these were exceptions; and his obligations as Attorney General were usually only to ride the circuit with the Superior Court—although he had also been given command of the militia. (As the result of a personal feud with the influential Langdon family and their friends, in early 1786 he declined reappointment as Attorney General, and resigned command of the militia.)

In June 1785, Sullivan became New Hampshire's Speaker of the House, and participated earnestly in the wrangling over problems of finance and trade. He was elected President (Governor) the next June, 1786, having the satisfaction of beating his personal rival, John Langdon, the incumbent President, by 51 votes.

Sullivan was forced to deal with a serious dilemma immediately upon taking office. Protests over the issuing of paper money escalated into the "paper–money riots", which came to a climax on 20September 1786, when rioters marched to a meeting of legislators in Exeter, seeking to intimidate them. Just as he had maintained discipline while in the army, he reacted with firmness, yet moderation. That night, Sullivan called out the militia, yet assured the mob he would see that no blood was shed. Next morning, 2,000 armed militia–men confronted the rioters, and took forty prisoners; the opposition collapsed. Sullivan then had the militia drawn up at either side of the road and rode between them, bowing to them as he did so. After this military ceremony was completed, the prisoners were made to walk between the lines twice, to have it impressed upon them what they would face if they were to try and take matters in to their own hands again. Finally, all of the prisoners were released, except five ringleaders, who were turned over for trial by Superior Court. John Sullivan had maintained law and order in New Hampshire; and Congress voted him their thanks "for his firm, zealous and decisive exertions"[96].

Another, though less serious, task Sullivan under took as governor, though with his usual diligence, was obtaining for Thomas Jefferson—and sending to him in Paris–a moose specimen with intact antlers, and with leg, thigh, and skull bones in the skin.

Jefferson was serving as U.S. Minister Plenipotentiary (Ambassador) to France; and, rather un–diplomatically, he wished to show the French naturalist Buffon that North

---

96   Whittemore. Op. Cit. p.203

American mammals were superior to those of Europe. When a cougar skin failed to impress, in consultation with Sullivan a moose was decided upon. In September 1787, a moose—dead–arrived in Paris, minus much of its hair. Jefferson, of course, was shocked by the cost, evidently ignorant of the fact that: sending a hunting party in to the wilds of northern New England in the middle of winter to kill a moose, and to move its carcass twenty miles through the forest; preparing it per Jefferson's specifications; and then shipping it across the Atlantic would be no easy matter. While Jefferson did have the bill paid—it was, after all, "someone else's money"— his acknowledgement of Sullivan's help was given with a tinge of sarcasm:

"He made the acquisition an object of a regular campaign, and that too of a winter one. The troops sallied forth in March—much snow—a herd attacked—one killed—in the wilderness—a road to cut 20 miles—to be drawn by hand from the frontiers to his house, etc. In fine he put himself to an infinitude of trouble, he did it cheerfully, and I feel myself really under obligations."[97]

Throughout late 1786 and early 1787, although Sullivan's detractors continued their venomous attacks, for the most part he was greeted with great respect, as he toured New Hampshire in the performance of his duties; and, despite the fact he had put down the money riots, he sided with the towns' opposition to the General Court's plan for paper money, so none was forthcoming. However, a stepped–up campaign of libel and slander against him—including charges related to his continuing attempts to be reimbursed for war expenses—did succeed

---

97 Edward, Brother C. "Jefferson, Sullivan, and the Moose". American History Illustrated. November 1974. p.19

in causing a close race between Sullivan and Langdon for the 1787 New Hampshire "Presidency". Neither received a majority of the vote; and, on 12 June, the Senate selected Sullivan, probably in thanks for his decisive actions during the riots.

First and foremost on Sullivan's 1787 agenda was prodding New Hampshire in to ratifying the U.S. Constitution, which was being worked on in Philadelphia. Fortunately for Sullivan, in this Langdon was an ally, throughout the contentious debating on the matter that went through 1787 and in to 1788; but, they still remained political opponents, and in 1788 it was Langdon's turn to win the presidency. Sullivan was successful, though, after a bitter battle, in getting New Hampshire to approve ratification, on 21 June 1788, the ninth state to do so—beating Virginia, to Sullivan's delight.

Prior to the 1789 election, Langdon resigned to become a U.S. Senator; and Sullivan ran against John Pickering, who was filling out the remainder of Langdon's term. As in 1787, neither candidate received a majority; so again the decision went to the senate, which once again decided on Sullivan. Thus, on 9 June 1789, Sullivan took the oath as President of New Hampshire, for the third and final time.

Then, just as the fall foliage makes October a glorious month for New Hampshire, events made October 1789 a glorious month for Sullivan—in retrospect, a "nova" of a month. Already a third term President of New Hampshire, his prestige—and income—grew even greater when with October came word that Sullivan had been appointed a Federal Judge for the District of New Hampshire by President Washington—with Senate approval!! Best of all, Washington came to visit New Hampshire that month;

and Sullivan was at the state line to greet his good friend and former commander–in–chief, "and then [proceed] with him to Portsmouth where a thirteen–gun salute greeted the President of the United States. The eager citizens lined Congress Street with 'all the crafts…ranged alphabetically,' the bells rang, and everyone 'hail'd (sic) their Deliverer welcome to the Metropolis of New Hampshire.' The visit was a splendid success with church services on Sunday, a trip on the water Monday,"–(do you suppose the two former comrades–in–arms might have reminisced, just a little, about their last trip on the water together, that freezing Christmas night of 1776?)—"and a gala ball Tuesday night at which Washington met 'a brilliant circle of more than seventy ladies.' The next morning President Washington left on his return journey."[98]

Almost symbolically, as the outburst of brilliance and exuberance created by Washington's visit began to fade away, so, too, did the star that was Sullivan. As a hint of things to come, rumblings of disapproval concerning his being both New Hampshire's President and Federal Judge prompted Sullivan to resign from the former before the completion of his term. Then, rapidly declining physical health, accompanied apace with increasing senility, precluded his performing his judicial duties after 1792.

(At this point, it seems almost obligatory for historians to attribute Sullivan's rapid deterioration to excessive drinking. However, while one can't doubt that a man named Sullivan, living during the hard–drinking time he did, drank his share of "toasts", it is also hard to believe that someone who had, over the years, worked so assiduously on so many complex problems, "never missing a day of work",

---

98   Whittemore. Op. Cit. p.223

would suddenly start imbibing enough to make him become incompetent within a matter of months. [Remember, while many scurrilous things were said of Sullivan during his years in Congress, and while serving in the Continental Army, never was he accused of drinking to excess— especially to the point where it impaired his ability to do his job.] It would seem that a more logical primary cause for his collapse, one that followed the course his did, would be some form of the progressive senile dementias—although, no doubt, "alcohol was involved".)

Never in great shape financially after his sacrifices during the war, Sullivan's fiscal problems really started to mount when, during the autumn of 1787, fire destroyed some of his mills, and a ship of his carrying beef to Bermuda was lost at sea. Then, as his competence declined, so did his ability to get payment of money due him–while, at the same time, his debts continued to grow. Towards the end, in the early 1790s, he had to sell some of his land; yet, he never became completely bankrupt, his inventory at the end listing his homestead—which included his modest law library–two farms plus some other land, two mills, and a press house.

Perhaps, though, in the end, Sullivan was not the un–lucky person historians feel obliged to call him. During his last years, Sullivan was surrounded and attended to by his loyal and loving family: his enigmatic wife; his three sons, who, although they had graduated from Harvard together in 1790, had the most un–gentlemanly tendency to start fights with anyone who spoke ill of their family; his married daughter, who lived nearby; and his parents, both of whom outlived him—his hundred–year–old father faithfully riding from Berwick to visit his ailing son. After all, nothing could be luckier than all this !!

It may or may not be true that Sullivan's "subordinate officers, when gathering for [his] funeral, were confronted by an undertaker who refused to bury their general until paid. The demanding undertaker changed his mind with alacrity when persuaded by a loaded pistol in the hand of Colonel Joseph Cilley (1ˢᵗ NH Regiment) and the possibility of needing an immediate burial himself."[99] What is known is that the cold New Hampshire winter weather that prevailed on the banks of Durham's Oyster River Friday, 23January 1795, prevented a ceremonious funeral for John Sullivan, age fifty–five. "Only" his family and some friends trudged through the snow to the family plot, where Major–General John Sullivan was laid to rest.

---

99 Ward, Ray. <u>March Into the Endless Mountains.</u> Waverly, NY: Weldon Publications, 2006. p.338

Afterword

Approaching Sullivan's simple, but stately, "Early Republican" house in Durham, New Hampshire, you think: "here lived a man who might today be known as an author of 'The Declaration of Independence', if he hadn't opted to fight for that Independence on the battlefield; one who crossed the Delaware by Washington's side, was the first American commander to work with the French as allies in war–and opened nascent America's western frontier to civilization". You wish you could have an intimate talk with him—if summer, sitting outside, overlooking the Oyster River; if winter, inside before a comfortable fire—discussing what he was feeling when he faced the oncoming British alone on Long Island, to give his men time to retreat–or thwarting an Indian ambush in the wilderness of New York State. You would end by asking him what he really thought of the Marquis de Lafayette—and John Adams and Thomas Jefferson–though that might be cause for a little more brandy!

Turning and walking to his grave–site, in a family plot

enclosed by a classic New England stone wall, with a somber, black wrought–iron gate, you ponder: Sullivan was a leader who risked making enemies to wage his own war on Congress, in order to ensure his men were fed and clothed as well as possible, whereas others might not have "made waves"; he was a true "soldiers' general", one who took the time and effort, after the Battle of Rhode Island, to successfully defend in a trial a subordinate officer who, if he had been found guilty, would have served as a scape–goat for Sullivan himself—even as other generals sneered.

Then—admittedly with tears in your eyes—you stand before Sullivan's grave, on a dark Fall day, and mutter to yourself, "You were a better man than most, John Sullivan!"

Bibliography

Adler, Jeanne Winston. Chainbreaker's War. Hensonville, New York: Black Dome Press Corp.,2002

Amory, Thomas C. The Military Services and public Life of Major–General John Sullivan. Boston, Mass: Wiggin and Lunt,1868

Adamiak, Stanley J. "Sullivan's 1779 Campaign". The Chemung Historical Journal. June, 2004

Bishop, Morris. "The End of the Iroquois". American Heritage. October, 1969

Cullen, Joseph P. "Brandywine Creek". American History Illustrated. August,1980

Edward, Brother C. "Jefferson, Sullivan, and the Moose". American History Illustrated. November, 1974

Esposito, Vincent J. The West Point Atlas of American Wars. New York: Frederick A. Praeger, 1959

Eyres, Lawrence E. "Sullivan's Expedition Against the Iroquios(sic)". The Chemung Historical Journal. December 1959

Fischer, Joseph R. A Well–Executed Failure. Columbia, South Carolina: University of South Carolina Press, 1997

Gottschalk, Louis. Lafayette in America. Chicago, Ill: Univ. of Chicago, 1975

Hammond, Otis G. Letters and Papers of Major–General John Sullivan. Concord, N.H.: New Hampshire Historical Society, 1930.

Ketchum, Richard M. "Men of the revolution XIII". American Heritage. August,1974

McCullough, David. John Adams. New York: Simon& Schuster, 2001

McCullough, David. 1776. New York: Simon & Schuster, 2005

"Officer in the Late Army". A Complete History of the Marquis de Lafayette in the Army of the U.S.A. Hartford, Conn.: S. Andrus and Son, 1848

Simister, Florence P. The Fire's Center. Providence, Rhode Island: Rhode Island Bicentennial Foundation, 1970

Spiegelman, Robert. "In Sullivan/ Clinton's Wake: Part.2" Chemung Historical Journal. March, 2005

Stephens, Karl F. "Color Guard". Sunday Journal Magazine. February 24, 1991_

Trevelyan, George Otto. The American Revolution. Longmans, Green & Co. 1912

Trussel, Jr., John B.B.. "The Battle of Brandywine". Historic Pennsylvania Leaflet. No.37

Walker, Anthony. So few the Brave. Newport, Rhode Island. Seafield Press, 1981

Ward, Ray. March Into the Endless Mountains. Waverly, NY: Weldon Publications, 2006

Whittemore, Charles P. A General of the Revolution. New York and London: Columbia University Press, 1961

Credits

Cover Portrait: Painted Ca. 1860, Richard Morell Staigg: Courtesy, Independence Historical Park Coll., Philadelphia.

Acknowledgements

I would like to thank Chris Eliades MD, New Hampshire surgeon and scholar, for his meticulous and helpful editing.

CPSIA information can be obtained
at www.ICGtesting.com
Printed in the USA
BVHW072200200120
569939BV00003B/273